THE
POWER
OF
BELIEVING
IN YOUR
CHILD

BOOKS BY MILES MCPHERSON

21 Jump-Start Devotional

The Power of Believing in Your Child

THE
POWER
OF
BELIEVING
IN YOUR
CHILD

UNLEASH YOUR POWER AS A PARENT
TO HELP YOUR KIDS BE ALL THEY CAN BE

MILES McPHERSON

BETHANY HOUSE PUBLISHERS
MINNEAPOLIS, MINNESOTA 55438

The Power of Believing in Your Child
Copyright © 1998
Miles McPherson

Cover design by the Lookout Design Group

Back cover author photo by Gerardy Photography, Escondido, California

Published by Bethany House Publishers
A Ministry of Bethany Fellowship International
11300 Hampshire Avenue South
Minneapolis, Minnesota 55438
www.bethanyhouse.com

Printed in the United States of America by
Bethany Press International, Minneapolis, Minnesota 55438

Library of Congress Cataloging-in-Publication Data

CIP data applied for

ISBN 0–7642–2078–0   CIP

I want to dedicate this book to

The young people who need someone to believe in them.

Never forget, with God, all things are possible.
All those who will believe in young people will win.
God can and will "do exceedingly abundantly above all
that we ask or think" (Ephesians 3:20).

MILES McPHERSON is president of Miles Ahead Ministries, an organization he founded to evangelize young people. In 1996 he launched Miles Ahead Crusades, which to date has seen over 62,000 in attendance and 10,500 young people give their lives to the Lord. Miles ministers each year to 250,000 young people through evangelistic and motivational presentations at school assemblies, youth conferences, and church-related outreaches.

Miles played defensive back for the San Diego Chargers from 1982 to 1985, during which time God gave him a burden to preach the Gospel to the lost—especially youth.

Miles joined the pastoral staff at Horizon Christian Fellowship in San Diego, California, where he was youth pastor from 1986 to 1992, and earned his Master of Divinity from Azusa Pacific University.

He has appeared on *Family Town Meeting* with Peter Jennings; a television special with Diane Sawyer; *Highway to Heaven*; TBN; *Focus on the Family*, and numerous television and radio programs across the country. He is also a popular speaker for DC/LA.

A C K N O W L E D G M E N T S

I want to give special thanks to

My parents for believing in me when I was a child.
The confidence you instilled in me has helped me believe that
all things are possible.

My wife and family who stood by me as I worked on this book.
I love all of you.

Jenny Gillespe for her tireless work and expertise.
Jenny, we did it!

Connie Neal for giving invaluable counsel that got
this whole project rolling.

C O N T E N T S

Introduction: Destined for Greatness 11
1. Destined to Turn Around 15
2. Destined to Live by Faith 33
3. Destined to Dream 53
4. Destined to Be Wise 73
5. Destined to Be Worthy 95
6. Destined to Have Courage 113
7. Destined to Stand 131
8. Destined to Be Pure 151
9. Destined to Lead 171
10. Destined to Shine 191

DESTINED FOR...
GREATNESS

A flight deck longer than three football fields stretched out in front of my vantage point a couple hundred feet above sea level on the bridge of the aircraft carrier USS *Abraham Lincoln*. The captain reeled off facts about his ship and crew. The *Abraham Lincoln* took seven years and five billion dollars to build. It carries eighty ultra-modern fighters, a cost of a few billion dollars more. Electronic gizmos pack the ship's control rooms, and, fully loaded, the *Abraham Lincoln* wields enough firepower to level half a continent.

And who steers this multibillion-dollar floating airport? Between chairs for the captain and the navigator stands a baby-faced nineteen-year-old, hands confident on the wheel, eyes on the horizon.

Seventy percent of the 5,500 crew members on the *Abraham Lincoln* are between ages seventeen and twenty, with an average age of nineteen. These sailors equip the ship for war—guiding planes for launch and landing, handling bombs, reading radar, watching over our national security, and willingly putting themselves in harm's way in world hot spots.

Sleep soundly, America. You can count on your kids.

"You should see these kids when we get them," the captain says, almost proud at the knowledge he hardly gets the cream of the high school crop. (Think about the guys who enlisted from *your* graduating class—teens who seemed to lack direction or options.) During basic training, though, they metamorphose. "We give them discipline, training, tell them they can do it," the captain says. "And they do."

That is the power of believing in a child.

If the United States Navy can take a raw recruit and a few months later hand him the keys to a multibillion-dollar nuclear-powered warship—and give similar recruits responsibilities all over the map—how much more can God remake a child entrusted to Him?

I have spent the past decade and a half since my retirement from professional football helping young people prepare for life through the power of the practical application of the Gospel. How? By helping them grasp God's special call on each of their lives. And by helping them grab hold of something that comes with that calling: their unlimited potential in God.

I have hope because in the Bible I read of God's hope for youth.

In this book you will hear about a young kid who took over the leadership of a country at age eight, and at sixteen brought about its spiritual reform. I will write about teenage men who witnessed the murder of their parents. Young men who were kidnapped and deported out of their country. Young men who, after all that, were still so committed to God that they refused to bow to a pagan god, even if it meant dying. I will write about a boy who was surrendered from the womb by his mother to be trained as a man of God. This same young man, who benefited from an adult mentor, became the spiritual leader of a nation. Later he anointed another teenager as king. I will talk about a young man who at seventeen was sold by his own family into a foreign land, only to later become a world leader. You will read about a young man who at fifteen survived the rejection of his much-loved father. He was banished to the wilderness with his single mother and left to die. Instead of giving up, he mustered the courage to care for his mom, survive, and birth a great nation. I will highlight a pair of teens who grew up in the same era, one to go on to be king, another to be a prophet. These godly teenagers later ruled nations and were miraculously saved from fire and lions.

Besides what I have read in the Bible, I have seen miracles in the lives of young people firsthand. I have seen troublemakers become peacemakers. I have befriended those who have had racial prejudice against me. I have seen young people overcome medical and family crises. All of these young people give me hope that anyone can be turned around *if only someone will believe.*

These are three things I hope you receive from reading this book:

1. *Insight to cherish your child as God does.* The Bible says that your child has been fearfully and wonderfully made. My goal is to help you see your child as God sees her, someone who was designed and chosen by God for something special. When you have that kind of insight, you can be your child's first and greatest supporter, a shelter your child runs to in times of trouble.

2. *Freedom from fear that your child will lose the game of life.* God can turn every negative situation into a productive one. And believing that fact is the beginning of supernatural transformation of the lives of you and your child. When you are free from your fears, you can help your child live up to his dreams rather than down to his nightmares.

3. *Courage to raise your child according to the promises of God.* Maybe you see failings in yourself and your parenting. You see flaws, big or small, in your child. Your child is in the midst of an intense spiritual battle, and there is only so much you will ever figure out on your own. When you have courage to believe in God's promises, you'll trust God to do the impossible in your child's life.

A child's greatest chance at life comes when he believes that God is unfolding a plan for his life, when he believes in his ability to adopt that plan, and when people—especially parents—gather around to support his pursuit of God's best. My prayer is that this book will inspire you to believe in God's calling and gifting on your child's life, and that you will unleash *the power of believing in your child.*

DESTINED TO . . .
TURN AROUND

" *There isn't any doubt about it, the human soul cannot go on forever in sin without some desire to free itself . . . conversion simply means turning around.* "

VINCENT MCNABB,
God's Way of Mercy

David once belonged to a gang. He carried a gun to school, used drugs, and bragged about being sexually active. Even so, he was a big teddy bear of a kid with a dazzling smile. No one thought he would die.

Yet one day I found myself conducting his funeral. I looked out to see his mother sitting in the front row, bravely listening to the story of her son's life. Behind her sat hundreds of kids who had come to say good-bye.

David's mother approached me afterward and tearfully thanked me for being her son's friend. At one time, she told me, her heart grieved for David and the destructive direction he had chosen in life. She had little power to influence him or change him.

But God did. David became a Christian at a church outreach during high school. By the time I met him, he had Jesus in his soul and joy in his heart. He was living a radically God-pleasing life and soon became a vital part of the high school fellowship I pastored.

David's cancer seemed to come out of nowhere. When the disease went into remission, David burst into life with fresh intensity, convinced he was healed. David became a zealous preacher—with a spin. He combined his love for music and disc jockeying with preaching the Gospel every chance he got. He made plans to go to Bible school and to work with me reaching kids like his old friends. We were going to make an album together, a kind of rap-Gospel thang.

But his cancer attacked again. His hospital stays became more painful and grueling, until his bloodred eyes and shaved head made his face barely recognizable.

Whenever I visited David, there were five to ten people waiting outside his room to see him. When he had turned his life around, the changes stuck because people surrounded him who loved him and taught him Jesus' love. He joined a Bible study and was mentored one-on-one. He figured out that a bunch of people believed in the Lord's work in his life. His closest companions were friends who loved God. As passionately as David had lived his heathen life, he now lived his Christian life.

His funeral became an opportunity to spread what he had learned about God and life, reaching out to hundreds of young people. Some were Christians, others were friends from the streets. Some came in suits, some in gang attire. Some drove up with parents, others in low riders.

Countless times David had watched me invite people to get to know God. On this day, he was the evangelist. David preached from the grave. He had prepared a slide show of his life to share and, even more to the point, a tape explaining his Christian faith.

Dozens of young people began to follow Christ that day, including David's cousin.

Because of what God had done in David's life, their time had come to *turn around*.

No matter how far gone your child seems to be, God offers a way back. For every kid going off in the wrong direction, God offers the chance to *turn around*.

THE NEW ABSOLUTES

RIGHT IS WRONG, WRONG IS RIGHT

I'm often asked why so many young people are in despair. David grew up in a setting where people expected him to get in trouble—the stereotypical Hispanic kid who became the stereotypical gang member. But the truth is this: We see David's whole generation in a crisis that ignores all social, financial, racial, and cultural boundaries.

I regularly stand before crowds of young people. Each time I see hundreds of children and teens trapped in the same dark hole where David once lived. I see these emerging adults stumbling around in a darkness ruled by drugs, violence, promiscuous sex, and despair.

God wants to illuminate their lives with His light and love. God wants to solve their problem, which has no earthly solution.

Drug programs, slogans, and campaigns are society's attempt to pull our youth from the pit. Society sees the dire condition of youth as a set of behaviors to repair. But the problem runs much deeper. Educating our youth about drugs, sex, and violence is well meaning, but it only addresses symptoms. It does little to change our children's hearts.

It's *inside*—in the heart—where most kids hurt horribly and where they are gravely misled. Recognizing that the pains of children and adolescents start on the inside is getting closer to the root of the problem. Most kids don't have the mindset to differentiate between right and wrong. Right has become wrong! Wrong is right! To many youth, coolness is ignoring parents. Ditching school. Getting high. Having a baby in high school—or even in junior high.

As adults, we hear rumors that "everybody's doing it." Well, peering through the eyeballs of youth, it looks like *everybody is*. They've been "doing it" in a variety of ways for a long time.

Seeing no other way of life, young people today possess a warped sense of what is normal, what is reality, what is good. For the most part, the adults in their lives are busy. They might be distracted parents, or lying leaders, or hypocritical preachers. To kids, most adults look too absorbed in figuring out their own lives to pull them from a vast wasteland of emptiness. If so many adults have no consistent moral standard to live by, why expect kids to behave? Who are their role models?

The world at large is no more help than the people in an average teen's immediate surroundings. Our media-saturated society makes celebrities out of people who are extreme, different, or weird. Serial killers get movies made about their lives. OJ Simpson's trial, the Oklahoma bombing, Jon-Benet Ramsey's murder, schoolyard shootings—these are the things that make a person famous.

Saddest of all, teens have no idea of how God sees their lives. Many have no idea they are acting in ways other than what God intends. God—more than any parent, teacher, or youth advocate—grieves that they chase actions and attitudes that destroy themselves. Though He believes in them, they cut themselves off from Him. That's sin. Sin is glorified in their lives!

We see these things happening to our teens. At the least, we get frustrated. We pace. We might scream on the inside—or outside. We inevitably do those parental lecture sessions we swore we'd never do. Sometimes we give up because we see no reason to hope.

People say that we have already lost this generation of teenagers—that we might as well focus on younger children. This generation reacts to our lack of faith in their future with apathy. They're chilled by the wet blanket we throw on their future. They're lured into hopeless complacency with little vision or promise.

Martin Luther King Jr. once said, "If a man has nothing worth dying for, he does not deserve to live." The Bible says, "Hope deferred makes the heart sick." When a heart becomes sick of being let down, it stops allowing itself to hope. Many young people have, therefore, quit looking to anyone to teach them, guide them, or act as a worthy role model because these expectations don't meet reality.

They begin to carve out their own realities and lifestyles. When little is expected of them, that is what they live down to. As Susan Littwin says in her book *The Postponed Generation*, "This is not a generation that protests or complains. This is a generation that avoids." Without a foundation to their lives that gives them consistency and certainty, youth choose to live only for today—and forget the consequences.

That puts us back at the beginning of the story, to new depths in a seemingly inescapable pit. The average kid who has become distant, apathetic, or mildly unruly needs a big touch of God's power to escape. And the one who falls as far as sexual promiscuity, drug and alcohol addiction, and jail time needs a genuine miracle of God to climb free.

IT'S NEVER TOO LATE

NOTHING IS IMPOSSIBLE

I have painted a bleak picture. As I look at this world where my own kids are growing up, despair would overwhelm me if I didn't hold to one truth: There is hope!

You may be concerned about the choices, big or small, your child makes daily. Your concern may have escalated to a worry that knots your heart. You may feel outright overwhelmed about the future your child faces. You are not alone. But realize there is hope. It's a real hope based on real promises from God, a hope that yields tangible results.

God's Word says this: "For with God nothing will be impossible" (Luke 1:37). All the problems I discussed above are—at their root—spiritual in nature, with answers found in the Word of God. In your most discouraging moments as a parent, you can realize God is on your side—and He is! As you hear how God has worked in the lives of youth, both in the Bible and today, you will be revived by the profound hope God offers you. And as you believe in and pray for your child according to God's will, all things are possible. You will agree with God's purposes for your child. You will help her to become all that God intends her to be.

If you are having a hard time buying that, I want to give you some practical steps toward changing how you think.

I. REALIZE YOUR OWN WEAKNESS

You may have tried everything in your power to change your kid. You've lectured, pleaded, prayed, manipulated, bribed—and still he is literally hell-bent on going his own way.

It's time to admit your weakness and inadequacy. No parent has limitless power to change all the circumstances in a child's life. That's a hard realization to face. But you *can* make a difference—a huge impact for good—because you can go to the Source of power, just as another parent did many years ago.

There was once a troubled father who in despair broke through a crowd to kneel before Jesus, publicly crying out in despair, "Lord, have mercy on my son . . ." (Matthew 17:15). Imagine this father's desperation! Risking public humiliation, asking for help, exposing his own inadequacies to help his son, the father sought his son's release from a demon that caused the son to throw himself into fire and water—completely self-destructive behavior.

"How long has this been happening to him?" Jesus asked.

"From childhood," the father answered. The father continued his plea to Jesus, "If You can do anything, have compassion on us and help us." It was almost a challenge to the Lord: "If You can do anything, will You help us?"

Jesus' response is what we need to drive into our minds: "If you can believe, all things are possible to him who believes."

What do you believe about Jesus' ability to help your child? Understand and believe this: Satan devises countless creative ways to keep your children on a path to self-destruction and to keep them away from God. But look at your children and know this also: God loves them and is completely aware of all they are going through. Never set limits on God's power, favor, love, and compassion for your child. Do you trust Him?

But wait, you say. I'm having trouble believing! I don't know if

I can handle this! My faith just isn't there yet! This desperate father answered Jesus with an honest and sincere heart: "Lord, I believe; help my unbelief!" Take your doubt, your fears, your lack of faith and spill them out to God: "Lord, I can believe up to a certain point, but this is so hard. Help me with my unbelief."

You can try to help your son or daughter on your own. Or you can let God answer your prayers in ways you haven't begun to imagine. Jesus commanded the demon to come out of that boy—and gave him back to his father, healed and whole.

2. IT'S NOT OVER TILL IT'S OVER

When you entrust your child to God, your faith often has to go back to basics: believing that God exists, that He is the giver of all good gifts to all who believe, that He indeed cares for you and your family as much as the Bible says He does.

Imagine yourself in the simple, humble position of the desperate parents of the Bible. God is as real now as He was then. Your need to relate to Him is at least as great. The human heart's cry for help hasn't changed. And just as God came near to the people of Scripture, God wants to help your unbelief, to strengthen your faith, to touch your life.

Maybe it has never once entered your mind to give up on your child. Your child's problems haven't overtaken you, or your patience can run a long way before it gets winded. But other parents—consciously or not—have said, "I don't know what to do about my child" or "I can't take this anymore" or "My child is beyond fixing." When things look utterly hopeless, that's when you pull out all the stops and prepare to go on offense.

When Jairus' twelve-year-old daughter was dying, he went to Jesus and begged (Luke 8). Jairus was a ruler in the synagogue, a man with religious and social clout and greatly respected in his community. Jesus, conversely, was despised by the very community Jairus represented.

But Jairus had reached the end of all hope. Casting away his pride like the worthless cloak of respectability it was, he fell on his knees in public to plead for his daughter's life.

You may have tired of crying out to God. You may feel your child's problems aren't big enough to bother God. Take heart and plead again with Him. Ask for help from the people who surround you. When you feel your son's or daughter's behavior has robbed you of respectability, it's painful to let others see your need. Jesus healed Jairus' daughter. The healing began the moment Jairus cried out for help.

3. YOU AREN'T ALONE. GOD HEARS YOUR CRY

When Ishmael was a young boy, he was left alone to die, kicked out of the house with his mother by Abraham, sent away to wander in the wilderness.

Abraham was in a bad situation. Hagar had been his concubine, Ishmael the resulting son. Now his wife, Sarah, wanted them out of her life. Hagar couldn't stand watching her son die, so she stuck him under a bush and turned away.

"And God heard the voice of the lad," Genesis 21 tells us.

You may have heard that God hears your cries, but sometimes that's hard to swallow. Well, Hagar had come to the end of her patience and strength and decided this was it for her and her son. No hope. No way out. Death in the wilderness.

But God heard a mother's plea and a child's cry for help. He intervened, saved them both, and fulfilled a promise He had made about Ishmael's life years ago to make of him a great nation.

God is in the business of fulfilling promises. Look through Scripture at how consistently He answers the prayers of hurting and frightened people. "For He will deliver the needy when he cries," says Psalm 72:12. "My heart and my flesh cry out for the living God. . . . O Lord, blessed is the man who trusts in You!" (Psalm 84).

The fact that the answer isn't immediate doesn't mean God is deaf to your desires. One night I got a phone call from a father whose son and daughter had both walked away from the Lord. He and his wife were loving, consistent parents who loved the Lord and their kids passionately. "They're lost!" he cried. "I don't understand how they could do this!" It was the anguish of a heartbroken father.

In time, both his children rededicated their lives to God. Were the years between prayer and answer tiring for my friend? Absolutely. Emotionally ravaging? Of course. But my friend learned the faithfulness of God. "Weeping may endure for a night, but joy comes in the morning" (Psalm 30:5).

GOD IS AT WORK

A CHALLENGE TO PARENTS

The Power of Believing in Your Child is written for you, the parent. My purpose is to turn the spotlight on our kids and God's purposes for them. That doesn't mean, though, that God has stopped working in our lives. By now it's no surprise to you that nothing will develop your spiritual muscles better than the workout you get parenting in today's world. So throughout this book we will stop and allow God to talk to us as parents, as people trying to follow God for ourselves. If we allow God to reveal to us things that will help us grow, we will find the strength to fulfill His call on us as parents.

As we consider God's ability to rescue and remake kids, think through the following questions:

Have you set your expectations too low? We all know that worrying is wrong. Worrying is a sin that says to God, "I don't trust you." In the same way, when we set our expectations too low for our kids, we're saying that we don't trust God and His promises. We're saying, "I'll settle for second best."

Remember the story of Peter walking on water? He and the other disciples were in a boat way out in the middle of the Sea of Galilee when a huge storm came up. They were being tossed about by dangerous waves when they looked out and saw Jesus walking on the water! Peter was eager to join Him, and Jesus' response was "Come!"

What if Jesus had said, "No, Peter. Stay in the boat. The waves are too high. You can't do this"? But Jesus said, "Come," and stretched out His hand. Jesus knew His own power and didn't limit His expectations for Peter's response! As a result, Peter believed in the impossible. He believed he could step out of his boat, out of his circumstances and former life, and walk on water!

God can call your child out of the storm-tossed boat, out of her former life to walk with Him across the water. God will not easily allow her to drown in her struggles. That's the God we believe in.

Do you believe in the impossible for your child? I said earlier that we are not fighting a battle that can be fought with snappy slogans and do-good campaigns. "We fight with weapons that are different from those the world uses," the Bible says. "Our weapons have power from God that can destroy the enemy's strong places" (2 Corinthians 10:4, NCV). Simple as it sounds, our primary weapons in parenting are prayer, the Word of God, and the wisdom to use each correctly. These are the most powerful weapons we can possess, because they allow us to align ourselves with God's purposes for our children. That's when miracles happen.

One day I was called to visit a young man in juvenile detention. "Suicidal, depressed, belligerent, and uncooperative . . ." was how the officer described him.

What he didn't tell me was that the young man was also a white supremacist.

I waited in a cell for him. As soon as he walked in, I noticed the marks on his wrist where he had tried to kill himself.

We talked for about ten minutes before it all fell apart. I mentioned the word "father." He blew up. His father had abused him and rejected him, leaving a kid seething with anger and rage, convinced he would never accomplish anything. While I tried to tell him that his heavenly Father loves him and wants to help him make a new start, he began yelling and cursing at me, telling me to get out and leave him alone. He was sure no one cared about him. He wanted to die.

As his tirade continued, I finally turned and walked out. I didn't know what to do. The boy's screams could be heard through the entire facility. I was embarrassed at having failed so miserably.

As I started to leave, I heard a guard say, "We just lost another volunteer." That comment enraged me. I turned around, determined to share the love of God with this kid and make him understand he has a future and a hope.

Has your child lost his or her volunteer? If young people are going to turn their lives around, adults must turn away from resignation and despair and commit to sticking it out with kids over the long haul, trusting God to do the real work. To get help, that young man had to overcome his prejudices against me, a black man. But I had a problem too. I had to overcome my discouragement and humiliation.

God was faithful. I returned, and eventually this suicidal racist surrendered his life to Jesus and turned around. God granted us a miracle.

Are you playing God? When I started out as a youth pastor, I wanted so badly to get young people to come to my Bible study that I picked them up, drove them home, called them, cajoled them, did just about everything short of bribing them. Unless giving them food counts as a bribe. Then I did that too!

When I finally talked to another pastor about the toll this frantic activity was taking on my personal life, he told me I was playing Holy Spirit. A psychologist might have told me I was enabling the kids' lack of responsibility. A teacher might say I was doing my students' homework for them. But what had happened was this: I had put myself in the place of God, trying to make something happen that only God can do.

Any change that takes place in your child's life will be the result of what God can do. Even though you are the most powerful earthly influence on your child's life—more powerful than peers, school, the media, sports heroes, and anything else you can think of—your role ultimately is limited and defined by God's own greatness. You are *God's tool*. You are not *God*.

Philippians 1:6 reminds us, ". . . being confident of this very thing, He who has begun a good work in you will complete it. . . ." Notice who began the "good work." God! There's a fine line between parenting that guides, teaches, models, and disciplines—and parenting that tries to take over what God is doing.

Nick's parents meant well. They prayed for him, loved him, and tried to help him get his life on track, but over and over they made one vital mistake: They bailed him out every time his money ran out. As a result, Nick depended on them for too much for too long. He stayed spiritually immature as well. When they finally realized what they were doing and set him free to handle his own finances, they saw an almost immediate leap in his maturity level, in ways both practical and spiritual.

As parents, sometimes we need to get out of the way and give God room to complete the work He began in our children's lives.

Are you helping your kids for your sake or theirs? Children's problems can become a staggering burden for parents. Troubled children are an inconvenience and a disruption. They wound your pride when you can't point at your kid and be proud. To relieve this misery, you may look for a quick way out. Buying, fixing, or denying away a kid's problems is a sign that you're laboring more to relieve your own pain than to find solutions for your child's long-term well-being.

It may seem unfair that your kid has to go through so much at your expense, but there is a *right* price to pay as a parent. As much as I advocate children being responsible for their own actions, we need to dive in with an active compassion for the circumstances around them that aren't their fault.

Children don't ask for broken homes. They don't ask to be molested. They don't ask for the increasingly violent, ungodly, and culturally ugly world they contend with every day.

Yes, hold them responsible for their actions. Help them to understand consequences. But help them fight the battles. Be honest enough to admit if you need to get your mind off yourself and look for God's will in their lives, not yours.

Are you prepared to make sacrifices? Parenting often means sacrificing your own desires, your own agenda, even your own plans. When God blesses you with a new baby, you know you're not playing house. You may not be able to afford the things you've dreamed of, or you may lose out on opportunities to travel or take more schooling. Your priorities will—and should—change dramatically. As your family grows, your time is tied up in your children's activities and schoolwork and needs. One of you may put a career on hold for a time to opt for the higher priority of rearing children.

Although parenting can seem like one string of sacrifices after another, be honest with yourself when your resources run low and your will to give and give again has been used up. Is there anything that competes for the time, financial support, or affection your child needs?

LOOK FOR GOOD

WHAT DO YOU SEE?

Look at your child and ask yourself what you see. A messed-up kid? An irresponsible flake? A rebel? A good-hearted kid who lacks even a speck of common sense? One who's lost and hopeless?

You might be surprised at how many parents look at their kids negatively. Maybe you aren't surprised. Maybe gloom is all you feel when you wonder if your child will ever change.

The Bible tells us in Philippians 4:8, "Whatever things are true, whatever things are noble, whatever things are just, whatever things are pure, whatever things are lovely, whatever things are of good report, if there is any virtue and if there is anything praiseworthy—meditate on these things."

Try applying that Scripture to your son or daughter. Look hard and discover what is good. Lovely. Pure. Praiseworthy. Make a list of what he or she has already come through. It may be a mild list. It may be a brutal list: drugs, pregnancy, rape, rebelliousness—but if you have been praying, something good has probably already come out of it. Has your child benefited from counseling, extra tutoring, special help programs? Has he or she survived physical injury? What positive things can you think of to fill your mind?

It's time to see what good things God is doing in spite of the heartache and trials you have endured, and realize that there is a master plan at work. Believe in God's work in your child's life.

SEE BEYOND

LOOK PAST THE IMMEDIATE CRISIS

Whenever I am asked to visit a high school, I find out what is going on there: atmosphere, morale, the socioeconomic environment. I recently visited a school with a beautiful new building and an incredible football team. Ranked first in the state of California, this school epitomized spirit and high morale. Over 1,800 students attended the assembly.

Immediately following, I noticed a young man lingering behind the group of teens that had come up to talk.

When we made eye contact, he approached me, leading me away from the crowd. Victor was one of the school's football players, and I figured he wanted to talk football with me. Suddenly tears started to well up. He told me about being the captain of the best football team in the state. He was popular, good-looking, in peak shape, widely admired—and miserable.

He couldn't live up to everyone's unrealistic expectations. He'd thought about suicide. This was a kid with pain for which he saw no solution.

As I shared the Gospel with Victor, I explained that as sinners none of us are worthy of any adoration. In front of God, we're all equal. Equally bad! Despite our badness, God accepts us because of Jesus' death on our behalf. Once Victor understood that the power of Jesus' love for him is bigger than his problems—and that no matter what, God accepts him and loves him for who he is—Victor received the Good News.

A year later I was invited back to the same school. Guess who the school president was? Victor. Guess who was heading up the Fellowship of Christian Athletes chapter on campus? Victor. Guess who was headed for Hawaii to play football for the university? Victor. Today Victor is a youth pastor intern at a local church. He communicates with young people the answer to the pressures that almost destroyed him.

Victor taught me to look beyond a kid in crisis mode to see a gifted young man trying to be too much to too many people. Ask God to give you a vision beyond the immediate problems that embroil you. God sees the bigger picture.

DON'T GIVE UP

WHAT'S A PARENT TO DO?

If it's true that kids can turn their lives around with God's motivating help, what can *you* do about it?

1. GO ON OFFENSE

Often when I speak at a school, I single out one kid to pick on, an individual who likes attention. My teasing pulls in the rest of the audience.

I was waiting for an assembly to begin at a Minnesota high school, scanning the crowd. There he was. He looked about 6'3", and upon my arrival he actually rolled out the last few bleacher steps onto the gym floor. He sprawled out over four seating spaces, drawing everyone's attention.

When I stepped out, the crowd was feeling good. So I started in by asking this kid's name. "Dennis," he answered, his body language defiant. I tried again. I needed a laugh real bad. Same cold response. Through the whole assembly, Dennis never cracked a smile. He glared at me nonstop with a straight, sullen look.

Later the principal asked me why I'd picked out this kid. I didn't know. The Lord led me. Then he told me Dennis didn't like black people.

That's when I went on offense. I asked if I could have some one-on-one time with him. The principal pulled Dennis out of class and we went into a private room. Remember I said he was 6'3"? Well, now he looked more like 6'6", and he had a huge scar running across the back of his head. After some small talk I asked, "Is it true you don't like black people?"

"Not all, just some kinds," he answered.

"What kind?"

"The kind who are lazy, sit around, collect welfare, and don't work."

"There's white people who live like that too," I responded.

"Well, I don't like them either," he said.

At least he was consistent. We talked a little longer; it seemed to go well. I encouraged him not to judge people by how they look.

That night I attended the school football game and found Dennis standing around with four other friends. One of them had a shaved head, and I wondered if he was a skinhead. Dennis was about to be tested, because I was going to talk to him until he made me leave.

Guess who followed me around during the rest of the game? Dennis and I walked, talked, watched the game, even broke up a couple of fights. We became friends.

Go after your kid the way I did Dennis. Pray that you won't be obnoxious, but when you sense you need to connect with your child, be a bit aggressive. Sit on the edge of his bed at night until he talks to you—and throw in a back rub. Take her out to breakfast so you can have one-on-one time. Don't be afraid to be strong with your kids. It says you care. It shows that you see the potential for change. In fact, it's the first step from you that most kids wait for.

2. TAKE CONTROL OF WHAT IS CONTROLLABLE AND LET EVERYTHING ELSE GO

You can't heal cancer, manufacture money to pay off debts, or reverse the effects of a car accident. But you can control how you *react* to these things.

You can develop a support system for you and your child—family, church, prayer partners, friends, counselors, whatever you need. You can take positive action toward solving problems. Ask for prayer. Seek advice. Appeal to friends and family for encouragement. Humble yourself, if necessary. Accept what you can't change, go after what you can, and put the rest in God's hands.

3. BREAK UP THE PITY PARTY

When your kids go through hard times, help them direct their thoughts. While you can be sympathetic, compassionate, and helpful, don't let your child or teen wallow in self-pity. There's a time to talk about things and a time to move on.

I'm not talking about suppressing real emotions that need to be discussed with a parent, friend, or counselor. But you can help your kids have a more hopeful view of life if you turn them toward the hope of remembering and acting on God's Word. Our hearts follow what our mouths speak, and God's blessing follows right choices.

Earlier we looked at Philippians 4:8, where we're told to think upon the good things in our lives. Right after that, the Scripture says, "I can do all things through Christ who strengthens me" (Philippians 4:13). If you can take your kids from the heartache of a trial to the victory of Philippians 4:13, there will be no room for self-pity and defeat in life.

4. REMEMBER: ALL BAD IS NOT ALL BAD!

God is the Master of turning bad into good. Jesus said, "If you have faith as a mustard seed, you will say to this mountain, 'Move from here to there,' and it will move; and nothing will be impossible for you" (Matthew 17:20). It doesn't take much, He was saying. Just a tiny seed of faith to cause something great to grow.

Throughout this book, I want to encourage you to look for the mustard seed in your child's life and then nurture it. That mustard seed may come in unexpected forms. What you might view as a weed could blossom into a mighty tree of faith!

Look at David, the young man at the start of this chapter. A lot of people thought his love for rap music was bad—a negative influence. But God turned it into good when He inspired David to use his music to reach other rappers. Music became David's ministry.

Trials are often fertile ground for that mustard seed. Even terrible experiences can be a seed of something good. Often it's up to parents to help a young person see this.

One summer at a youth camp, a young girl came forward and blurted out that she had been molested by her father. That day she needed someone to hear her pain. In the months and years that followed, she needed a compassionate voice to tell her that God can use great pain to bring great good. Part of that good is being able to minister to others who face similar devastation—exactly how the Lord later used this young girl. She needed the right God-inspired counselors to help her move from pain to gain.

5. WORK TO BELIEVE AND ACHIEVE THE IMPOSSIBLE

Go back to the verse we looked at in the beginning, Luke 1:37: "For with God nothing will be impossible." It's a matter-of-fact statement spoken to encourage a parent facing huge trials ahead: Mary, the mother of Jesus.

When an angel of the Lord told Mary what would soon happen in her life, those are the words he chose to sustain her. "No matter what's ahead, Mary," he was saying, "believe that nothing is impossible with God."

God had a special plan for Mary's Son. He has one for your child as well.

Because Jesus came and died for sin, He cleared the way for God to turn your child's life around and fulfill one of the Bible's finest promises: *"Therefore, if anyone is in Christ, he is a new creation; old things have passed away; behold, all things have become new"* (2 Corinthians 5:17).

Don't quit praying.

Don't quit believing.

God can make all things new for your child.

CHAPTER TWO

DESTINED TO...
LIVE BY FAITH

Faith means being grasped by a power that is greater than we are, a power that shakes us and turns us and transforms and heals us.

PAUL TILLICH

Four girls in matching dresses, shiny shoes, and toothy smiles stepped up to the front of the church. It was midnight, Christmas Eve, in a season when people flock to church in uncommon numbers expecting something special and extraordinary. This night they weren't disappointed.

The sisters—ages six, seven (twins), and nine—were introduced, then proceeded to recite from memory the entire fifty-third chapter of Isaiah and Isaiah 9:6–7. No stammering. No hesitation. No looking for cues from Mom or peeking sideways to read a sister's lips. With clear, sure eyes, they looked straight out at the huge audience and shared God's uplifting Word.

The congregation burst into joyous applause. Some cried. Everyone felt as if they had just witnessed an Olympic gold medal victory.

I happen to know that these girls don't just look good on the outside. Their faith is real on the inside, where it counts. They are happy, sensitive to spiritual things, and caring toward others' needs. They are impressive not only in intelligence and poise but in attitude. Their parents don't have a dazzling social life, but they are committed to raising their daughters in a loving, spiritually enriching environment. They use a formal curriculum that calls for them to recite eight verses three times a day—and the youngest memorized as much as her older sisters just by being around them. Nightly devotions with their parents include singing, praying, studying the Bible, and learning hymns. Missionaries often stay with the family, or visit and share in their devotions. The girls look for, expect, and see answers to their prayers.

Now, maybe you think this family's regimen is overkill. No one but you can decide what's right for your family. Even so, your expectations can either limit or unleash your children's spiritual growth.

HAVE FAITH
DESPISE NOT YOUTH

I don't believe these four remarkable young girls are unusual—not in the sense that they have a superspiritual potential beyond that of other young people. God created each kid unique, special, with one-of-a-kind gifts. Yet all young people—yours included—have the ability to memorize God's Word and live out its truth.

You might have a shiny-shoed kid who makes everyone in church smile. Or you might have a son who only gets to church because you're still big enough to corral him into the car on Sunday morning. You may feel ashamed when you think how distant your daughter is from God. Maybe church, God, and faith seem far off for your whole family. Yet faith is a gift God wants our children to possess.

Is it hard to believe that God has designed your children to believe and trust in Him, to know His voice? Could it really be that someday your son or daughter will follow God without your help and input? Easy to accept or not, your child has a call from God.

If God is calling our children, we have to wonder why more don't heed Him, especially given the two choices: (1) Seek God, and He blesses life with purpose and direction. Or (2) Live without Him, and life is ultimately meaningless. The results of a wrong spiritual choice are startling. In a study of college students who had attempted suicide, nearly nine out of ten said that life seemed meaningless, even though more than nine out of ten of those suicidal students had good grades, an active social life, and a decent family environment. What they lacked was purpose and meaning.

Why would a child or teen choose emptiness rather than God?

For starters, our culture dislikes God. Sure, life is full of spiritual fads and God-talk, but an obedient relationship with the true God of the Bible gets a cold response in most places.

That's enough to make most kids struggle with staying close to God. The chill grows when kids see Christians labeled "narrow-minded" or "intolerant" or "unloving" for upholding biblical principles in areas like sexual morality, homosexuality, and abortion. It's not easy for a kid to go against the mainstream, especially when the stream is a roaring river! The Bible says the road to destruction is wide and attracts a huge crowd, while the road to life is narrow and few take it. Even a son or daughter who wants to stay on the road to life can't help but notice the big crowd on the other side and feel a tug.

Although the world is the primary threat to your child's faith, the church, regrettably, is frequently part of the problem—despite also having the solution. In spite of the fact that the apostle Paul told Timothy, "Let no one despise your youth, but be an example to the believers in word, in conduct, in love, in spirit, in purity" (1 Timothy 4:12), Christians often ignore young people's spiritual potential. It's easier to assume "Kids will be kids," to write them off as too immature to connect with God.

Studies of people who quit church find that close to half of all Americans withdraw from active religious participation at some point in life. Adolescents are most at risk of quitting. While some churches try to attract teens with entertainment or fun-and-games, teens cite the lack of opportunity for *significant* spiritual growth as a primary reason for abandoning church attendance. Few youth are fooled by a faith that doesn't tackle the hard "whys?" of life.

Even if your child belongs to a rip-roaring youth ministry with age-appropriate services and classes, he won't follow Christ as an adult without a sense of the church as a whole. Most church structures siphon youth off into their own programs, where they rarely join in the adult world of church as capable sisters and brothers in Christ. A church that doesn't provide youth with genuine opportunities to worship and serve alongside adults will watch its youth drift away. They won't see how they fit into the bigger church.

Kids who struggle with acceptance and identity—and that's most of them—also get hard knocks at church. Sermons say, "God has chosen the foolish things of the world to confound the wise. . . ." We claim that God can use anyone, that He lifts up the meek and weak, that inner beauty counts more than outward. But we esteem the most athletic, popular, physically beautiful, talented, and accomplished kids. In spite of our good intentions, churches fall into the trap of being more impressed by worldly accomplishments than by simple faithfulness.

The church and society—there's plenty of blame to go around. What about us—the parents? How do we stunt our kids' spiritual development?

Kids learn far more at home from what they see than from what they hear. They watch our actions more than they listen to our words, especially when it comes to spiritual things. Mom and Dad can portray godly people at church or in front of their friends, but kids know what goes on at home. They aren't fooled. The Bible calls that parental split-personality "double-mindedness," a sin that makes a person "unstable in all his ways" (James 1:8). It makes for a confusing family.

Children resent hypocrisy. They'll wonder why we can be so nice and good to people outside the family yet so meanspirited and unspiritual at home—especially when Mom and Dad are church leaders. "All will know that you are My disciples," Jesus said in John 13, "if you have love for one another." Sometimes as believers we're so busy loving one another outside the home, we forget that love begins at home.

Or if we teach our children to do the best they can, to succeed in as many areas of life as possible—and *then* squeeze God in when it's convenient—their spiritual development will fall short. It's nice to see our children excel in school and sports, make money, and be socially successful, but equipping them spiritually has much greater long-term benefits. To paraphrase Jesus, what does it profit our children to succeed in every other area of life, if in the end they fail toward God? (Mark 8:36).

GOD HAS A PLAN

DESTINED FOR GREATNESS, BY FAITH

There's good news, however. There isn't enough time, the writer of Hebrews says, to tell us about all those who through faith "subdued kingdoms . . . stopped the mouths of lions, quenched the violence of fire, escaped the edge of the sword, out of weakness were made strong, became valiant in battle . . . received their dead raised to life again. . . ."

You might read through this list of amazing feats (Hebrews 11) and think, *That's fine for all those Bible heroes—but not for my child.* The point, though, is that these things are possible for all who believe—including children and teens!

Throughout the Bible we meet young people God chose to be kings, queens, military leaders, warriors, political advisors, spiritual leaders, and national heroes. For the most part, those He chose weren't extraordinarily gifted, skilled, wealthy, or beautiful. The great attributes they may have gained were the result of God's work in their lives.

God often explained to parents ahead of time the mission He had for a child. An angel told Joseph, for example, that his son, Jesus, would save His people from their sins. When Hannah cried out to the Lord for a son, she vowed to dedicate him to the Lord's service all the days of his life. God answered her prayer by giving her Samuel, who responded to God's call as young boy and grew up to become a prophet to kings and country. Not only were the parents forewarned in both cases but the calling on their sons' lives began during childhood.

Or look at the prophet Jeremiah. One day the Lord clearly said to him, "Before I formed you in the womb I knew you; before you were born I sanctified you; and I ordained you a prophet" (Jeremiah 1:5). Jeremiah responded, "Behold, I cannot speak, for I am a youth." As in, "Hey, God! I'm too young for this!" But God's response was the same then as it is today when He calls a kid to step out in faith: "Do not say, 'I am a youth,' for you shall go to all to whom I send you, and whatever I command you, you shall speak. Do not be afraid. . . ."

Jesus wasn't afraid when He stayed behind at the age of twelve to converse with the elders in the synagogue. When His parents found him after three days of anxious searching, He said to them, "Did you not know that I must be about my Father's business?" Though Mary and Joseph didn't completely understand what all this meant, they took Him home, helped Him grow "in wisdom and stature and in favor with God and men," while Mary "kept all these things in her heart."

David was still a teen when his brothers met with the nation's leaders, trying to devise a plan to defeat Goliath. David, a shepherd boy, got the lowly job of bringing provisions for his brothers. When David realized no one had the courage to face the bully, he volunteered. King Saul immediately scolded him, "You are not able to go against this Philistine to fight with him; for you are but a youth" (1 Samuel 17:33).

David, who had already killed a bear and a lion while defending his father's sheep, wouldn't be denied. "The Lord . . . He will deliver me," he said. You know the rest of the story. Goliath didn't stand a chance against this bold, faith-filled teenager.

Joseph was a teenager when he dreamed great and mysterious dreams about leading his people. He even had the audacity to tell his parents and siblings that he would one day rule over them. His brothers didn't take that news well—they sold him into slavery at the age of seventeen. Young Joseph ended up in a foreign land where God blessed him and fulfilled the visions of his dreams (Genesis 37–50).

Esther, the young Jewish maiden who captured the king's heart, became queen of Persia. Her heritage remained a secret until her people faced annihilation. Esther stepped forward and revealed her identity, risking her life to plead for mercy for her people. She was brought into a foreign kingdom "for such a time as this" and met the challenge with courage and wisdom, saving her people.

Josiah became king of Judah at the age of eight. Imagine your third grader—the one you can't trust with the lawn mower—having a kingdom to run! Josiah had help in the early years, but Scripture tells us that by the age of sixteen Josiah "began to seek the God of David" and "he did what was right in the sight of the Lord" (2 Chronicles 34–35). By the time he was twenty, he was instituting reforms to return the country to a godly course. This young man faced pressure from every side, but his faith gave him the vision and courage to rule wisely and to honor God with his service. When he died, the nation mourned him as a premium-quality king.

In some of these cases, these young people recognized God's call on their lives and went about fulfilling it before their parents clued in. In most cases, though, parents are a big part of encouraging and teaching their child to hear the voice of God.

As a parent, you'll need to reckon with the fact that God has a plan for each child that is more important than whatever you have planned apart from Him. God's plans require parental participation, not control. Prayer is the most powerful way you can participate, because when you give up your own desires and pray for God's vision, you can spot God's will and support your child in following His leading.

Your child may never be a king or a warrior or a prophet, but the pressures facing young people today require equal courage—a quality of character that comes only by seeking God firsthand. In God's eyes, these examples aren't unreachable goals. They're models of what you can dream for your child.

SPIRITUAL GROWTH

WHAT DO YOU REALLY THINK ABOUT YOUR CHILD?

Every summer Miles Ahead Ministries teams up with a summer camp in the San Bernardino mountains to give inner city kids a week in the woods. We draw kids from San Diego and Los Angeles, some of whom have never been out of the city.

One day at the pool, I noticed a young man praying. In the middle of the day, when most of the kids were in the water having fun, this guy was off by himself praying. What kind of kid is this? What planet is he from?

Curious, I took some time to get to know him. I discovered a sensitive, friendly fourteen-year-old with a deep, sincere love for the Lord and His Word. He loved to talk with God and made prayer a priority. I admit that at first I wondered if he had some serious problems or was socially maladjusted. To the contrary. He had lots of friends and treated both adults and kids his age with respect. He played basketball and baseball and had a good social life.

This guy had maturity uncommon for his age. He had no one to impress. He simply loved God and had his priorities right.

When you meet kids who are truly devoted to the Lord, who are walking in the Spirit and seem to have a mature spiritual perspective toward life, what do you think? Are you skeptical? Do you believe it could happen? Do you want that for your kid?

Again, a few questions for parents. By the way, if you find yourself not liking your answers, God has grace to help you along, one step at a time. And as you receive His grace to grow, you can pass that same grace on to your child. God doesn't just believe in your kid. He believes in you. Think about the following:

Do you believe your child can grow spiritually from where he is now to where God wants him to be? Think about the quality and quantity of spiritual growth you expect of your child. You might be surprised at your own skepticism. Many parents decide early on that their kid is still young . . . there's time . . . let him be a kid for a while.

Sometimes we mistake the process of sanctification (the Bible term for growing up, the process of getting there, what we reach for in this life) with absolute perfection (completion, the end result, what we'll reach in heaven). A child who loves and seeks God won't be perfect, because all children—all human beings—struggle and disobey from time to time. But a child who has a genuine personal relationship with God learns early that God loves him, that God forgives sin and helps him get up and go on. Perfection isn't the goal for today. Today's aim is a heart willing to grow and be matured by the Lord.

Do you limit how you pray for your children's spiritual life? In chapter 1 we talked about Peter walking on water and what that implies about limiting your expectations for your child. Similarly, you can limit how you pray for your children because deep down you believe some goals are impossible. You might settle for a "keep my kid out of trouble, God" or bland prayers for "safety" or "success." God wants to do those things. But you can also stretch out, believing and praying for your child to be used by God. You can ask God to do the mighty and marvelous works God wants to do in his or her life.

Raise your child's sights by praying with her for what God wants to do in her life. When a child sees you praying and believing all things are possible with God, she begins to believe it too.

Are you willing to get your hands dirty and be involved in the process? One night a couple expressed to me their concerns for their two sons. The boys' friends were challenging their beliefs and making fun of them for going to church. The boys were being asked questions they couldn't answer.

I suggested the parents have the boys write down their questions, and, as a family, research the answers in the Bible. The two brothers would grow in faith, the family would get some "together time," and the boys would have something to share with their friends. It would also put them on the offensive rather than the defensive. When they felt ready, they could even invite the other kids over and have a discussion night.

There was only one catch: this plan required the parents get involved and do their homework. The dad responded rather defensively, "That would mean I would have to know the answers. I don't know if I could do that."

"Look," I said, "just do the best you can. The point is, do it— get involved, get your hands dirty, go into the trenches with your boys. God will honor that." Then I was a little blunt. "And if you aren't willing, you can't expect to have godly kids."

As a parent, prepare yourself for this awesome job. Even when that means extra study time in the Word or getting involved with your kids' friends, you won't regret it.

FEED ON THE WORD

ARE YOU TENDING YOUR FLOCK?

When I visit people around the country, I aim to encourage the children of the ministers who host my visits. When I talk to these kids about their spiritual lives, we discuss what their prayer time is like, how their Bible study is, if they're involved in any ministries. I gauge their interest in spiritual things but I let them know I'm not there to grade their performance. I genuinely want to know how I can encourage them.

Prayer is the best way to get to know anyone. Sometimes I talk with these kids out on the sidewalk in front of the church, in the church office, in a car. Wherever we end up, I ask these new friends to pray for the people coming to hear me speak. I ask them to pray for their own friends, family, and for me.

So I listen to people's prayers. I listen to see if they use Scripture when they pray, and if they have a burden for lost souls. I pay attention to see who prays with authority and experience, who seems shy and hesitant. Gaining this insight gives me direction in how to minister during my visit.

The tables were turned on me one day. As I walked out of a wedding with my pastor, he joked with my three children. He asked them to recite John 3:16. They were eight, ten, and eleven at the time. Of course, I started sweating, eager to impress my pastor and thinking, *You'd better get this right, kids, or it'll be a long time till Christmas.*

The verse eventually trickled out through giggles and stuttering. But it made me stop and consider the spiritual state of my own children. Good shepherds should know the condition of their flock. My most important flock is my family. If I take so much time to get to know where other people's kids are at spiritually, I'd better know where my own are.

Over the next week, try to answer the following questions: *Do your kids read their Bible daily?* (I admit it's hard to get kids to do much of anything every day. But put it this way to them: They eat daily. Feeding on the Word is their spiritual food.) *Do they pray for others in trouble or in need?* And finally, *Do they have their own personal relationship with the Lord—one that isn't forced on them by you?*

Your most important sheep are your children. Get to know where they stand with God.

ALLOW GOD TO SPEAK

FAITH IN ACTION

Once you've determined the "state of your flock," you might want some suggestions for putting that knowledge into action. Here are a few that I have found to be across-the-board effective in helping your child encounter God.

1. CREATE OPPORTUNITIES TO BUILD YOUR FAMILY'S FAITH

Two wealthy families made mission trips to Hungary one summer for their vacation. They spent two weeks cleaning toilets, eating strange foreign food, sleeping in less-than-plush accommodations. This was jarringly different from their usual vacations to million-dollar homes in Aspen or the Caribbean. The teenage daughters probably felt the difference the most. There were no boys, no makeup, no TV, music, parties, shopping, or a need to dress up. Nothing but hard work and daily Bible study with Mom and Dad.

The girls loved it. With each rust-stained toilet they cleaned, their hearts grew more sensitive to the Lord and to other people's needs. The girls began to ask for more time to study the Word with their parents. The family members pulled together.

Once they returned home life picked up its normal pace. But even though TV, parties, the good life—their usual distractions—beckoned, the girls stayed focused. Their level of interest in spiritual things had never been so high. Countless other families have taken similar mission vacations and seen the fruit stick as well.

2. MAKE SPIRITUAL HIGHS THE SPIRITUAL NORM

When your child has that kind of spiritual experience that jump-starts faith—especially one that jolts a kid who has grown up in the church but never really owned her faith—bottle that energy before it fizzles away.

A friend of mine was having trouble with his teenage son. The boy was stubborn, sullen, and selfish, and he was making everyone else's life miserable. One weekend the boy went—under duress—to a youth retreat with their church. He came back on fire for God! His attitude around the house changed dramatically as he made efforts to respect his parents and get along with everyone.

My friend worried because after a week or so he noticed signs of his son's excitement waning. He wanted to know what he could do to keep the fire burning.

I reminded him that the Holy Spirit is the One who keeps the spiritual fires burning. As a parent, you can pray for that to happen. But I also encouraged him to build a fresh relationship with his son. Trying to put spiritual expectations on a kid without establishing friendship and respect is a mistake. As Josh McDowell says, "Rules without relationship will be broken." The son needed to know his parents care for him for his sake and not their own selfish desires.

I edged this dad toward spending quality time with his son, requiring nothing but love. I told him to make his son laugh, become a friend as well as a father, plan things they could do together. Once the son realized his dad was on his side, his advice and spiritual mentoring would be better received. Since things had been so difficult between them before, the dad doubted how much he could influence his son. But now they have regular Bible studies together at the son's request, and the Lord is keeping the spiritual fires burning.

You can't rely on your youth pastor, your church's youth group, retreats, camps, trips, and so on, to do long-term spiritual training. Those are all good tools, but you are the one constant factor in your child's life.

3. DON'T IGNORE A CHILD'S DESIRE FOR BIBLE STUDY, CHURCH, AND SERVICE

"Mommy, I can't go to bed. We didn't have devotions." The weary mom looked at her charming eight-year-old daughter and sighed. Did her child really want a Bible study—or was this a ruse to stay up longer?

It's both. Most kids relish the idea of time spent with Mommy and Daddy reading the Bible, talking, praying. Sure, they can manipulate you and stall bedtime, but then it's your job to schedule the evening so that there is time for the Bible study.

Romans 10:17 says that "faith comes by hearing, and hearing by the word of God." In order to build faith in your children, they have to hear the Word. Bible study can be simple. In our family, we sit down together and read a passage of Scripture. Then I ask, "So what?

What is the point of the story? How does it apply to your life?" This always generates discussion.

When children are young, they hunger for the things of God. It is we—the old, busy, tired parents—who need to ask God for the discipline and desire to feed our children spiritually. Even teens are more spiritually receptive than we ever think. Rattling around in the head of even the coldest kid are deep questions about life. If you've never studied the Bible together, go in reverse: talk first, Bible second. Ask your son's or daughter's opinions about significant issues, and let the conversation roll from there. Then jump into the Bible when your child's curiosity warms up.

4. BE AN EXAMPLE

The Bible says, "Train up a child in the way he should go, and when he is old he will not depart from it." Your child can't be trained unless you are, and you can't ask him to do what you won't do yourself. Children need to see living illustrations of godliness, and the best people to paint those pictures are parents.

One powerhouse preacher, Samuel Shoemaker, once said, "Most people are brought to faith in Christ not by argument for it but by exposure to it." If you want your kids to study the Bible, stay in fellowship, and serve the Lord by serving others, they need to see you do it first. All the arguing, nagging, worrying, and complaining you can do accomplishes nothing compared to your real-life witness.

You've heard the old saying that "you can lead a horse to water but you can't make him drink." I don't believe that. I can not only lead a horse to water but I can make him drink—and drink a lot. All I need to do is run him around in the hot sun to create an irresistible thirst, and then bring him to the water. Guess what? The horse drinks.

It's that way with our kids. When we do our job as parents by modeling real faith, God will create an irresistible thirst in our children, one that in time will cause them to take in living water in astonishing amounts.

5. CHALLENGE YOUNG PEOPLE TO PRAY BIG PRAYERS

When I was being nurtured as a new Christian, my teacher, Sherman, always picked someone out of our little group and asked him to pray. If we grumbled, he had a stock answer: "We need prayer and you need practice."

Recently my wife and I decided to buy a fixer-upper house, which was like paying money to get a list of endless repairs and cleaning chores. A friend helped us scrub the laundry room floor with what turned out to be a flammable solution. Suddenly we heard a crash and smelled smoke just as the fire alarm went off. I ran into the room and saw flames dance across the floor. Thinking one of the cleaning rags had caught fire, I tried to stomp out the fire. Too late, I discovered I had put my foot into a container of burning fluid. The whole fiery mess flipped up toward my face and leaped onto my hair. My head was burning as I ran backward out of my house, bumping right into my wife. She screamed, threw me down on the ground, and started yelling, "Roll! Roll!"

Smoke and flames were coming off my head as I rolled and rolled through the damp grass. As soon as the flames were out on my body, I went back inside to put the flames out in the house. Meanwhile, my wife and children were screaming, "Get out! It's going to blow up!"

We survived with a minimum of damage to both house and hair. But later, when I asked one of my daughters what she thought, she answered, "Satan is trying to hurt you because you preach the Gospel." I wanted to assure her of God's protection on our lives without undermining her spiritual concerns. So I gathered my family, and we committed ourselves to praying about Satan's attacks on us. Armed with the Bible promise that Jesus will never leave us nor forsake us (Hebrews 13:5), our kids learned to face a physical and spiritual threat through prayer.

Don't be afraid to challenge your children to pray. As they grow older, let the issues grow with them. Call family prayer meetings when something important comes up. Don't leave them out. Teach them to keep a prayer journal. Let them see how faithful God is to answer their prayers. It's part of their spiritual training and faith building.

Maybe prayer is a long forgotten habit in your house, something you did with your child when he or she was small. If you can't imagine where to start, pray for the things you and your son or daughter have no solution for—the things you can do nothing about but pray. God is not a vending machine, a dispenser of goodies for every request. But God wants to act in your life through what you pray. Start small, be faithful to pray, and let Him be faithful to you.

It can also be difficult to get your whole family focused on praying together, especially if your kids are of varying ages. It helps our family to sit in a circle and pray, one person at a time. We use the following outline, going through each item and giving each child a chance to pray for one thing. No, it doesn't spell anything—but it hits the high points of prayer:

A—Admire or thank God.

W—Wait in silence.

C—Confess sin.

I —Intercede for others.

P —Petition for ourselves.

A—Admire or thank God again.

I ask each child, for example, going around the circle, to thank God for one thing. Then we continue on down the list. It keeps us focused and our heads together, greatly enhancing our prayer time.

6. HELP THEM GET PERSPECTIVE ON THEIR PROBLEMS

No surprise to most parents: teenagers are egocentric. Their problems can become so all-consuming that they completely lose perspective. Let them start there. Let them pray that way and seek God's answers. Find Bible passages that fit their personal problems. But move them along. Young people, for example, are prone to dwelling on negative circumstances without ever stopping to consider their blessings. One antidote is to encourage them to minister to people with bigger problems than theirs.

Carrie is a Filipino teenager. She's been homecoming queen and plays varsity all-star basketball. Like all teens, she has suffered her share of worries, anxieties, boy troubles, and conflicts with her parents; the list goes on.

Though she was a regular at a Bible study at my house, she seemed clueless about what God really had to do with her life.

I often took kids to a little town in Mexico to minister and to take in supplies and clothing. One weekend Carrie joined us. The poverty of the town—a few shacks, really—shocked her. Barefoot children with ragged clothes, no electricity, no running water, stifling heat in the summer and near freezing temperatures in the winter. We spent several hours giving out clothing and sharing the Gospel before we were invited into a small home.

Carrie and another boy joined me as we walked into a small, neat room with one bed, no windows, and a dirt floor. We knew we had more food in our lunch bags than the family had in the small ice chest nearby. A tired-looking young woman in a tattered dress did her best to make us welcome. With a baby in her arms, she offered us food and drink. We realized that the water she offered us had to be carried in from a fifty-gallon drum outside. We stayed about thirty minutes, leaving behind some food and supplies.

Suddenly Carrie's problems fell into perspective as she realized how much God had blessed her life, and how much He could use her to bless others. What a difference that one trip made in Carrie's life!

7. TEACH YOUR CHILDREN COMPASSION

Ministering to the less fortunate won't only help change your child's perspective. It will teach compassion as well.

In the canyons of surrounding neighborhoods, we see many Mexican immigrants walking or riding bikes through the streets, looking for work, hoping to pick up a few dollars for food. Entire communities of families live out in the open with no electricity or water—usually within a mile or so of wealthy neighborhoods.

Throughout the Gospels, we see Jesus feeding the hungry and ministering to the sick. Jesus didn't pity the poor. He had compassion. Pity looks down at needy people and hopes they get help. Compassion gets down with people, empathizes with their pain, then tries to do something about it.

My children constantly ask to help the people in the canyons. They have given some of their most precious toys and other possessions to the children in these communities. We also take our kids to feed the homeless. As a family, we sponsor a child through Compassion International. Learning compassion is learning to follow Jesus.

8. ALLOW GOD TO SPEAK THROUGH YOUR CHILDREN

One Sunday after an evening church service, a thirty-year-old father and his two sons came to talk with me. The father, battling alcoholism and separated from his wife, desperately needed prayer. I prayed for him, but I also challenged him to turn his whole life over to God. He surrendered his life and asked Jesus to save him. He wept with his two boys and made a commitment to get help for himself and his family. Then he admitted that he came that night because of his six-year-old son.

A year later, this man is still sober and walking with God. A six-year-old boy had enough faith to lead his dad to the Lord.

As adults, we look for teachers and leaders who can give us wisdom and insight. These teachers might be right under our noses as God allows our children to exercise their faith by ministering to us. "Out of the mouths of babes . . . ," Jesus said.

9. KEEP BUILDING SPIRITUAL MUSCLES

If you have older, mature kids who are walking with the Lord, encourage them to keep growing. Praise them for the blessing they are, but provide ways to let them build spiritual muscles.

Help your kids identify and use their spiritual gifts. In 2 Timothy

1:6 Paul reminds us to "stir up the gift of God which is in you. . . ."

When I pastored a high school fellowship at a large church, I put those kids to work, and they loved it! I challenged each one to find a job and commit to it for a set amount of time. Some jobs were practical, like setting up chairs, running sound systems, cleaning up, bringing food, planning events, welcoming newcomers, making announcements—the list is endless.

Others committed to leading worship, praying for specific needs, or organizing prayer groups. The more mature kids taught the Bible to younger ones as we set up one-on-one discipleship. They planned street witnessing nights, convalescent home visits, fun times, serious times, serving times. They were active and excited as I encouraged them to expand their vision and meet new challenges. Some amazing things came out of those kids, and I know that many today are still dynamically serving the Lord.

DESTINED TO BELIEVE

In a way, this whole book is about faith. It's about your faith in your child, and your child's faith in himself. But those little faiths root in ultimate faith: a living trust in God. As you seek to grow that special brand of belief in your son or daughter, watch throughout this book for things that triggered spiritual growth in other kids. Maybe you'll see your child mirrored in one of the stories.

Faith is a gift God wants our children to possess. With faith, there are no limits to what they can accomplish and no room for empty, unsatisfying lives. Faith will fill our children with hope, purpose, and the power to fulfill God's destiny for their lives. Faith will give wings to their dreams.

"Blessed are those who hunger and thirst for righteousness, for they shall be filled" (Matthew 5:6).

CHAPTER THREE

DESTINED TO...
DREAM

"
You see things and you say, 'Why?' But I dream
things that never were and I say, 'Why not?'
"

ROBERT KENNEDY,
quoting George Bernard Shaw

Her mother was the only white person living in the projects. As a young girl navigating her way through the maze of red brick buildings, Debbie often felt scared and alone.

Even though she'd lived there all her life, Debbie never quite fit in. Thirty identical brick buildings of ten apartments ringed this crowded Connecticut community where residents shared garbage dumpsters, play areas, parking space, and walkways. Day and night people hung out playing music, talking, dealing drugs, messing around with no particular purpose. Eighty percent lived on welfare.

In the hot summer, music blared, and lack of air conditioning guaranteed every window would be open. During winter, snow covered everything, but that didn't stop people from hanging out. Debbie's family never had a car, so they pulled their groceries home in a cart across the field behind the complex.

Her father, an African-American, was never very involved with his family, and he left for good when Debbie was sixteen. She and her brother and mother constantly struggled to survive. Christmas brought presents only if her mom's friends pitched in with used clothes and toys. Even so, Debbie lied to other kids about her presents to make herself feel better.

During her fourth, fifth, and sixth grade years, Debbie walked to school under police escort. Her light tan complexion made her the target of racist blacks who hated mulattos. Other kids kept their distance, leaving her to play alone most of the time. At night, rocks came hurtling through her bedroom window, carrying their message of hate and violence. More than once, her family's front door was kicked in and her mother assaulted.

In seventh grade, something changed. A small seed of determination grew until Debbie decided she'd had enough and started fighting back. She made up her mind she didn't have to accept this life. She could do something about it. She began to dream about moving out of the projects.

Her dream grew. It became the motivating force that helped her stand up to other kids. Eventually the fights stopped. She found a job and began to develop a plan.

Even though Debbie had little outside influence and encouragement, she had a dream for her family and her life that would not be denied. She had no one to rely on. She knew no one who had made it out of the neighborhood. But she had a dream.

Her persistence paid off. Debbie worked every job she could find until she could buy a car. She even worked alongside her mother at the local Burger King. In time, Debbie left the projects behind and built a new life. Today she has a beautiful family, with three wonderful children, and lives in a warm, comfortable home. I should know.

Today she is my wife.

Debbie's world was filled with poverty, racism, violence, and despair. Yet a dream flickered within her, waiting to ignite. Debbie's faith in God came later, but she looks back now and knows that He is the one who put the determination in her heart.

All young people have dreams burning within. They have visions of doing something bigger than life, of making a difference in the world. While many factors have to be in place for a dream to be fulfilled, the reverse is also true. In order for a dream to be quenched, something must be wrong.

LET THEM DREAM

ROOM TO DREAM

The poet W. B. Yeats wrote,

> But I, being poor, have only my dreams.
> I have spread my dreams under your feet,
> Tread softly because you tread on my dreams.
> (from "He Wishes for the Cloths of Heaven")

Those lines echo the plea of our children. As young people, they come to us—parents, the church, society—with little more than their dreams. Our job is to recognize those dreams and step softly, lest we trample the ideals that will energize the next generation.

We also need to identify *how* a person's dreams get stomped on, spotting the situations and attitudes that destroy a young person's ability to dream and to set goals.

Once we discuss a few of these dream killers, I want to talk about what we as parents can do to fight back.

DREAMS ARE KILLED WHEN YOU DON'T SEE GOD'S GREATNESS

At a conference for professional athletes, educator Cindy Tobias taught about four brain types. After dividing each type into groups, she asked questions. My favorite was, "What do you like most about God?" My group was categorized as *concrete random*, which basically means competitive to the core. So naturally we wanted to come up with the best answer.

One group said what they liked most about God is that He is orderly and organized. Another answered that it was His love. Another cited His forgiving nature.

Our group was excited. We knew we had the best answer, and we wanted to win the contest—a contest that was purely a figment of our brain type's competitive imagination. The attribute we liked and admired most about God was that He does big things! When our spokesperson announced our winning answer, we all cheered, to the audience's total bewilderment. They didn't get it. But we won the contest.

We snuff out dreams if we limit our vision of who God truly is. God does big things—even in the lives of young people. They need room to dream, permission to dream, and opportunities to dream. And we need to help them pursue their dreams.

DREAMS ARE KILLED WHEN LIFE IS A NIGHTMARE

I visited an alternative school in the lower Midwest for sixth through eighth graders. Each student there had a record of disciplinary problems and mental instability. Kicked out of every school they had ever attended, they were getting one last chance before being permanently expelled from the district.

When I asked the principal to profile the student body, she looked tired. Out of forty-two pupils, she told me, only two lived with their natural parents. The rest were constantly being bounced around among foster homes. Most had been abandoned by their parents and were heavily involved in gangs. Some had been put up in a home until the bills came due, then they had to move on. A few had been expelled for carrying a concealed weapon. Drugs, sex, abortions—the whole range of tragedies that afflict the young were present in that one small group. Remember, these were junior high–age kids, and already they had reached the last stop.

The woman who arranged the assembly stood nearby. She began to cry, just listening. When I asked the principal what I could do or say to best help, she looked at me and said, "These kids have never in their lives seen anyone achieve anything positive or have a dream come true. Help them believe that it is still possible to work for something and get it."

These children may have been the extreme fringe of society's failures, but I know they aren't that different from the rest of our young people. Even kids from pretty homes who have less obvious problems struggle to hang onto their dreams. Our society doles out discouragement, negativity, and pain in heavy doses, with no respect for social and economic status. When young people watch so many of their peers fail at life, they see no hope for the future.

DREAMS ARE KILLED WHEN PEERS CUT YOU DOWN

One afternoon I conducted a class for a dozen teenagers. I asked them to tell me what they wanted to be when they were twenty-five years old. One by one they said the same thing: "I don't know."

I couldn't believe it. I couldn't get one student to admit to a dream for the future. As I went around the room and told them to throw something out—*anything*—what I discovered was frightening. No matter what each kid said, someone else laughed or made fun of him. Each jab was accompanied by a list of reasons why that individual could never achieve such a ridiculous goal, complete with a list of personal shortcomings. *Yeah, you could never do that—you're too stupid . . . you're too ugly . . . you're too weak*, and on and on.

Those who dared stick their necks out quickly retreated. Being laughed at killed their dreams. Peer pressure can kill the motivation to succeed. Misery truly loves company.

DREAMS ARE KILLED WHEN YOU'RE AFRAID TO LIVE

Teenage death is usually self-inflicted or related to drugs, gang warfare, or stupid accidents. Sometimes I think kids just give up and let reckless living take its toll.

Daytime talk shows are full of kids who claim to accept death as part of their tough lifestyle. They brag about their dangerous activities and claim nothing is worth living for, no dream is worth pursuing. They boast about not fearing pain or death. To them, tomorrow doesn't exist. Even kids from good homes buy this garbage—because it's "life on the edge," cool and exciting.

These kids aren't so brave and tough that they're not afraid to die. They're afraid to live.

They're intimidated by failure. They're afraid of never seeing their dreams realized, so it's safer not to try. They haven't been taught that real living is experiencing and learning from failure, that true success is measured by one's personal growth in the pursuit of a dream. They aren't convinced that God is real and bigger than life's obstacles. They don't believe that He cares enough to handle the growth and that He always has a next step in mind for them.

Every kid has a dream inside. It may be buried underneath an enormous pile of pain, frustration, and negative influences, but it's there. You just need to know where to look and how to dig it out.

WHAT DOES IT MEAN?

BELIEVE IN THE DREAM

There was a seventeen-year-old young man named Joseph who faced all of the above obstacles. As a young boy he dreamed of greatness. But no one around him believed the dreams, thought they were God-given, or considered they could come true. Even his beloved father rebuked him. His brothers resented his dreams so much that they made his life a nightmare. Talk about peer pressure! He was betrayed, sold into slavery, lied about, thrown in prison, and almost killed. Yet his dreams also made it possible for him to survive. They were ultimately fulfilled because, you see, God had a plan for this young man. God planted those dreams in Joseph's heart to motivate him toward his destiny.

I want you, as a parent, to be convinced that God will do the same for your child as He did for the Joseph of the Bible. He encourages all of us, His children, to pay attention to our dreams, to look to Him for their fulfillment, and to trust Him to help us rise above adversity. Take the time to go through God's Word and find the Scriptures that tell us just that. (Joseph's story is in the book of Genesis, chapters 37–50.) After you have been encouraged as a parent, share those Scriptures with your children. Here are few to get you started:

> Delight yourself also in the Lord, and He shall give you the desires of your heart. (Psalm 37:4)

My friend Sherwood Wirt likes to quote this verse and say, "Do you want your dreams to come true? Then follow the Lord and watch Him do it!" God puts desires, hopes, and dreams into our hearts. After all, He created us! His will is that they be fulfilled. Satan's will is that they be destroyed. If we allow God to mold and shape our lives, if we will stay close to Him, if we "delight" in Him, then He will bring our dreams to life—in a manner beyond our expectations.

> For we are His workmanship, created in Christ Jesus for good works, which God prepared beforehand that we should walk in them. (Ephesians 2:10)

God has a plan for each of us and our children, something He is preparing us for. If you can believe that God made your child exactly as he or she is, to do something special and unique that is suited to that individual personality, intelligence, and emotional makeup— then you will appreciate the uniqueness of your child's personality and dreams.

> Now to Him who is able to do exceedingly abundantly above all that we ask or think, according to the power that works in us, to Him be glory. (Ephesians 3:20)

What a great Scripture! God will not only fulfill our dreams but He'll do beyond what we could possibly expect or imagine. Tell your kids. God is not limited by our puny imaginations!

> And it shall come to pass afterward that I will pour out My

Spirit on all flesh; your sons and your daughters shall prophesy, your old men shall dream dreams, your young men shall see visions. (Joel 2:28)

Prophecy, dreams, visions—all forms of communication from God. He wants us to experience them all. Dare to dream dreams for your children, and ask God to give them vision and words of freedom for their future. You know it's His will because it says so in His Word.

Not that I have already attained, or am already perfected; but I press on, that I may lay hold of that for which Christ Jesus has also laid hold of me. (Philippians 3:12)

The apostle Paul longed to become what God had already planned for him to become. Jesus Christ had already "laid hold" of the future for Paul, and Paul didn't want to miss anything! What do you think God has prepared for your child? The army recruiting slogan promises a young person: "Be all that you can be." Maybe, maybe not—in the army. But God can actually make it happen. All our kids are destined to be successful dreamers. It's our job to help them believe it and to "press on."

Where there is no vision, the people perish. (Proverbs 29:18, KJV)

Dreams are not a luxury or an indulgence. Our kids need a vision for life. God's Word says that without a plan, we perish. Hopelessness destroys. Parents provide encouragement and opportunities that will help young people hear God's call and find direction for their lives.

Now faith is the substance of things hoped for, the evidence of things not seen. (Hebrews 11:1)

Joseph was the ultimate dreamer. He didn't just dream. He *expected* his dreams to come true. That's what I want to see in our young people—an expectant desire, an anticipation that needs no evidence other than the dream itself. If the dream is from God, it will require faith to see it fulfilled.

Joseph's faith didn't allow him to become paralyzed by his circumstances, even though he had good reason to roll over and quit. After all, what good could come of the anguish Joseph endured when his brothers rejected him, harmed him, then sold him into slavery? What could come from years in prison, false accusations, and betrayal?

Joseph's faith enabled him—forced him—to hang onto God and his dreams. Each hardship and painful event were part of the Master's plan to move Joseph to Egypt and facilitate his rise to power as second in command. Ultimately, the life of his family and his people were entirely dependent on Joseph's benevolent authority and power.

His dreams had been fulfilled "exceedingly, abundantly," beyond anything Joseph expected.

THE ROAD TO SUCCESS

SOMEONE HAS TO OWN THE ZOO

Immediately following a school assembly, a teenager ran up to me with tears in his eyes. "I want to play football," he said. "But my father keeps telling me I can't. He says I'm too small and I wouldn't be any good. He won't even let me try. I know I can do it. Do you think I can play football?"

He went on for a couple of minutes. The entire time he was talking, about ten other kids circled around me, asking for autographs, thanking me for coming, or just clamoring for attention. He didn't care. He was oblivious. He was waiting for someone to tell him, "You can do it. You aren't a failure."

He needed someone to believe in his dream with him. He wanted to believe that his dream was worth having. Whether or not he had the talent to play football isn't the point. He had a dream and the desire to try. Anyone who has succeeded in life knows that desire is 90 percent of the battle.

I realize that this boy's father may have been perfectly well-intentioned. He may have been trying to protect his son from what he saw as certain humiliation or bodily harm. What he didn't realize was that he had laid a heavy, frustrating burden on his son by denying him the opportunity to dream.

Are you a dream killer? Answer these questions and see if you recognize yourself:

Do I discourage my child's interests because they don't interest me?

Am I unwilling to help implement dreams?

Do I allow fear or worry to influence my attitude?

Am I unwilling to take my child's dreams seriously?

Do I avoid bringing up the subject?

Do I act bored if my child brings it up?

Do I just plain not care and show no enthusiasm?

Am I unwilling to invest in my child's dreams?

Have I neglected to pray about it?

If you answered yes to any of these questions, ask yourself the whys and whats about each circumstance. Then it's time to make some changes. This may require some sacrifice, or at least a reorientation of your thinking.

My oldest daughter, Kelly, loves animals. Anything that's dying she'll try to save. One day when I asked her what she wants to do when she grows up, she said she wants to own a zoo. I had to think about that. It sounds like a pretty lofty dream. But who am I to kill her dream? After all, someone has to own the zoo. Why not her?

Don't ever get caught being a dream killer!

BECOMING A DREAM BUILDER

I have some friends whose daughter has for several years shown an interest in horses. Even after suffering a traumatic injury when bucked from a horse, she had no fear about riding again as soon as she healed.

My friends aren't "horsy" people, but they began to recognize a real dream in their daughter's life. She was willing to work after school with no pay at a scruffy little ranch near their home, mucking out stalls, grooming animals, cleaning equipment, helping other riders—just plain working hard for the privilege of being around horses. She made friends in the horse community and is well respected as a hardworking, honest kid.

Her parents worried about her safety, about the time she was spending, about the time *they* were consuming driving her to and fro. They watched her start saving for a horse and began to sweat what it was going to cost.

These parents could have stomped out her dream early on, but they recognized that God might have a purpose in all this. So, in faith, as they can afford it, they are investing in her dream, doing what they can, and praying together as a family to help her realize her goal of owning and training a horse someday. They've even discovered they enjoy this new venture! Through their daughter's dreams, they have contact with new people and new ideas that have broadened their horizons.

Ask yourself if you're a dream builder. But before you go through the following checklist, realize that the process of pursuing a dream is more important than the goal. The dream may change, but the lessons will remain. My friend's daughter may someday lose interest in horses and move on to other things. But in the meantime, she's learned to work hard, be responsible, and pursue a goal with determination and patience.

Have I invested in my children's dreams?

When they begin to talk about ideas, do I get excited?

Do I initiate conversations about their dreams?

Do I help them prepare to fulfill their dreams?

Do I spend time researching the subject with my child?

Am I patient when their dreams change?

Do I help my kids associate with other successful dreamers?

Do I pray with them about their dreams?

VISION FOR LIFE

DREAMS HAVE THEIR OWN FUEL

One evening I watched a documentary on teenagers and guns, featuring a seventeen-year-old boy who had been shot in the neck and lost the use of his legs. A former gang member, he once bragged about accepting death as part of everyday life. Before the bullet hit, he had no direction, no goals, nothing that mattered.

Now he is driven by a dream he will pursue against all obstacles and odds. He has a reason to live because he is obsessed with willing his legs to walk again.

Refusing to accept the verdict of doctors, he wakes up every morning and begins the grueling exercises that keep his muscles toned. He won't listen to discouragement. Every day, faithfully, he pursues his dream.

It's tragic that it took a stray bullet to give him a purpose for living. A desire to live and an ability to dream surely resided in his heart before, but his dreams were buried beneath misconceptions of what is cool.

Young people who have no vision will perish, either from lack of hope or the consequences of reckless behavior. The number one killers of white teens are drunk driving and suicide. For African-American and Hispanic teens, it's homicide. Both have the same root cause: lack of vision for life.

Dreams have their own fuel. A kid with a dream will need no pushing to pursue his passion. If your child has no dreams, make it your goal to help him discover what God has buried in that young heart before it grows too hard to find.

SELF-TAUGHT DREAMER

DREAMERS TAKE THE DRIVER'S SEAT

Keron's family emigrated from Trinidad. Growing up in New York City, he acquired an intense love for trains, especially the subway. Every day he hung around subway stations, talked to conductors, learned the lingo, and rode the trains. He dreamed of operating one himself.

Not content with dreaming, Keron took command of the A train on 207th street one Saturday afternoon by impersonating an off-duty conductor. Using a fake ID, he picked up the required regulation equipment—including the brake handle, safety vest, and key—and for three and a half hours, took thousands of passengers on a ride that was, for him, a dream come true.

Keron was thrilled! He took the train through Manhattan, on into Brooklyn and back. He drove the correct speeds, read the tunnel lights accurately, stopped right on target at the platforms, and operated the doors smoothly to let passengers on and off. He successfully conducted the train through eighty-five stops. His joyride came to an end when he barely broke the 20 mph speed limit, tripping the automatic brakes and alerting the authorities. Now the courts have to decide what to do with him.

I'm not justifying what he did, but the truth is he didn't set out to commit a malicious or violent act. He wanted to fulfill a dream. There are wiser ways to go about it, but Keron has all the ingredients of a good dreamer. Successful dreamers want to be in the driver's seat. They have their own way of doing things. They've thought through how they want to do something, they rehearse it over and over in their minds, and then they act it out. Put a basketball in the hands of a kid who wants to "Be like Mike" and he'll hang his tongue out, dribble between his legs, spin, and act as if he can really fly.

Dreamers pretend they are in the big game, singing at a concert, or being a mom. Whatever their dream, they work at it, study it, and prepare themselves for the day they actually do it. Just as Keron rode the subway every day, observed procedures, learned how to do it—then did it—successful dreamers are self-educated.

DIRECT THE DREAM
TURN NEGATIVES INTO POSITIVES

What do you do with a young man like Keron? Unfortunately, he's been in some trouble since the train incident, but at the time, his neighbors, teachers, and friends described him as decent, considerate, and smart, although underachieving. There were, of course, those who thought he should be sent to a juvenile detention center. He broke the law and endangered lives.

I see it a little differently. Keron possessed a good desire that played out in a bad way. The solution isn't to destroy his dream but to direct it. You have a young man with an irresistible love for trains and the obvious intelligence to learn to run them. Why not put that to good use? Give him a job, but make him work without pay for a while to compensate for breaking the law. He'd be a great worker because he loves what he's doing. If he had been channeled into something constructive, he might have avoided some of the trouble that came later.

Dreamers are also preoccupied with their dreams, no matter how unique or different they may be.

Matthew had a habit of drawing coffins in his spare time at school. This seemed more than a little strange to his teachers and classmates. They worried about what his preoccupation with death and burial might mean. But one day an intuitive teacher introduced Matthew to the neighborhood mortician. Matthew found his niche. He learned to work alongside the mortician, and today he owns two large cemeteries in California.

Proverbs 22:6 tells us, "Train up a child in the way he should go. . . ." Implied in this familiar verse is that each child is unique and needs to be guided and accepted according to his individual personality, temperament, inclinations, and gifts. And all these things rolled together add up to a dream.

FIT THE FRAME

REAL DREAMS

I'm not going to lay all this on you without giving you some practical ideas. So here we go:

GET A BIGGER FRYING PAN

Sixteen-year-old Charlie visited his Uncle Mike in the mountains to go fishing for the first time. Charlie arrived fully equipped with new fishing gear. The lake was like glass, the sky was blue, the birds were singing. A perfect day.

After paddling their canoe out about fifty feet from shore, they cast their lines. Each caught several good-sized fish, and Uncle Mike was feeling satisfied about Charlie's experience, until he noticed something strange. While Uncle Mike stored his catches in the basket that hung off the edge of the boat, Charlie threw all his back into the lake, even though several were fairly big fish.

Uncle Mike finally asked, "Son, why are you throwing them back? They're certainly big enough to keep."

"They're too big for my frying pan," Charlie replied.

Uncle Mike responded with an incredulous laugh, "Then get a bigger frying pan!"

The possibility of a dream being realized is sometimes hard to accept, because the "frying pan" where it needs to be cooked is too small. The opportunity can be right in front of you, but given your circumstances or tools, you don't see any way to implement it. So you throw the dream away and settle for something smaller.

Debbie, in this chapter's opening story, had never seen anyone make it out of the projects. Accomplishing her goal seemed impossible because she had never see it done. But she made it because she enlarged her "frying pan." She found jobs, multiplying her options and holding onto her dream. Now she can encourage others and tell them it can be done!

If your child has a dream that seems impossible, find others who have done the very thing they dream about and get them together.

Find examples for them of what is in the realm of the possible. Show them how to get a bigger frying pan.

DON'T LET THE PROCESS HINDER THE DREAM

No dream is too big. But the process of getting there can be intimidating.

When I was a nineteen-year-old sophomore, my dream to play for the NFL was given a huge boost when I met Terry Jackson of the New York Giants at a football camp. Like me, he played defensive back. We sat in his room one afternoon and talked for a couple of hours about the things guys at football camp talk about. We talked football, then more football, and then some more football!

The time I spent with Terry changed me. I was able to see and touch my dream through him. I realized that regular people who identify their talents and work hard see their dreams come true. I believed I had the talent. I wasn't afraid to work. On that day the size of my frying pan tripled as I saw that my dream was a real possibility. The process of getting there no longer overwhelmed me.

If your young adult is floundering in pursuit of a dream because the process is too intimidating, seek out and introduce her to people who have achieved similar goals. Initiate conversation about goals, then research the possibilities together. Give her an assignment to take one step toward her goal, then make her follow through on it.

BUILD CONFIDENCE

HARD WORK REQUIRED

All of us know people who succeeded because they worked hard—not because their natural gifts put them at the top of the pile, but because they had something better: a disciplined work ethic. "He who is slothful in his work is a brother to him who is a great waster," Proverbs 18:9 tells us. Ecclesiastes 5:3 says, "For a dream comes through much activity [or hard work]."

Teach your children to work hard and consistently. The super-talented are few. Most winners are those who counted the cost of success and were willing to pay the price in hard work.

As you look around for a role model, look at God. In Genesis, chapters 1 and 2, God performed the incredible task of creating the heavens and the earth. He set the ultimate example of a consistent work ethic:

1. He stated His plan to create the heavens and the earth (Genesis 1:1).

2. He worked on one project at a time, until it was finished (Genesis 1:2–31).

3. He inspected His work to see that it was done properly before moving on to the next project. (Genesis 1:12, 17, 21, 25, 31.)

Let's examine each step and see how it applies to you and your children.

1. Identify the dream. Just as God identified a specific goal, you can teach your kid to do the same. Even prophets were instructed by the Lord to write down their dreams. Here's what He told Habakkuk:

> Then the Lord . . . said: "Write the vision and make it plain on tablets, that he may run who reads it. For the vision is yet for an appointed time; but at the end it will speak and it will not lie. Though it tarries, wait for it; because it will surely come, it will not tarry" (2:2–3).

A missionary friend of ours, Kathy Rogers, works with high school students in eastern Europe. One of her team's activities is to take these kids on a three-day retreat designed for "dreaming." After spending some time getting to know one another, the kids are left to themselves for a few hours and instructed to write a list of dreams. They are told to make believe that God could use them to do anything. Since it's "make-believe," there's no pressure to limit themselves to what seems possible.

A year or so after one of these retreats, Kathy went through the list with her group. She discovered the kids had actually experienced half of the things they wrote down—things they thought they could never do. By the time God gets through with them, the rest of the list may well be checked off too.

When I speak at schools, I similarly invite young people to write down their dreams. If their dreams can't be articulated, they will never become a reality. They'll remain a feeling or unformed longing. Writing down an idea turns feeling into reality and helps a young person have a clearer view of the dream.

Encourage your child to record his dreams in a diary or journal, then pray about them. Even if he doesn't achieve his original dreams, the pursuit will develop character that will be helpful for the rest of his life.

2. Keep the vision before you, completing it one step at a time, until it is done. During my years with the San Diego Chargers, the guy with the best hands was Peter Holohan. We called him "Sweet Pete" because of his amazingly soft hands and his ability to catch the ball in weird positions. I had to cover him almost every day in practice and I was awed by his skill.

Besides the fact that he had huge hands, how could he catch so good? "Be the first to see the ball," he says, "and don't take your eyes off it." No matter where Sweet Pete ran his route, he made sure he saw the ball first and kept his eyes locked until the ball landed safely in his hands.

Help your child identify her goal, then keep her eyes on it until it is achieved.

Like we said before, the process of achieving the goal can be scary. A young person who wants to be a doctor can be discouraged by the prospect of twelve-plus years of expensive education. But breaking down the process into steps—pre-med, medical school, internship, residency—makes it feel manageable. Finish one step at a time while keeping the ultimate goal clearly in mind.

Isn't that how God created the heavens and the earth? He knew what the end result would be. But even God completed one step, one day at a time, until the goal was achieved: Creation! The Bible is clear that successfully accomplishing "little things" leads to bigger and greater things (Matthew 24:24–26). Each small step is part of the larger goal. When you complete all the steps, then you achieve your dream.

3. Make sure each step is done properly. When you give your kids a job to do, do you check their work? Delegation without evaluation doesn't accomplish the goal.

Whenever my kids tell me they've finished a chore and want to run out and play, I tell them I'm going to check it out first. That usually sends them running back to do a better job. I have a saying about this: "People do what you inspect, not what you expect." When your child knows he's accountable to someone for the quality of his work, he tries harder and is more likely to do it right.

You can help by going over the task. Such as, "Katie, is this bathroom clean enough to pass inspection?" If she doesn't get it right, patiently walk through the task with her. "OK, is the toilet clean? Are the mirrors polished?" Let the child gain a sense of pride for a job well done.

Accountability starts with parents, but eventually kids will need to evaluate their own work. They need to learn to do their work right because it's the right thing to do, not just because someone tells them to. They need to become accountable to the Lord. "And whatever you do," Colossians 3:23 teaches, "do it heartily, as unto the Lord and not to men."

God's example to us is that He also took time to inspect each stage of His work. After pronouncing it "good," He moved on to the next step. When the whole of creation was complete, He looked at everything He had made, and saw that, "indeed, it was very good."

When the principle of doing each step right is established in childhood, it carries into young adulthood and gives kids confidence to reach for their dreams.

KEEP ENCOURAGING

GOD'S ADVOCATE

When I wanted to play in the NFL, I kept friends and mentors around me who believed in me. A guy named Gary Reho was one of them. He designed flyers to promote me and sent them weekly to NFL teams. His flyers literally paved my way.

One of my coaches tried out for an NFL team but didn't make it. He kept the contract that was never signed as a memento, and showed it to me one evening. Touching that contract was actually a thrill. It gave me a tangible connection to my dream, something I could feel with my hands instead of my imagination. I became more determined to have a contract of my own—signed.

In 1982 I became the first player in the history of the University of New Haven to get drafted to play in the NFL. Several years later one of my brothers ran into my head coach, who had said I would never make it. The coach admitted that what happened defied the odds. He was surprised.

My encouragers kept me working hard, hoping and praying. If I had had only discouragers around, my dreams to play in the NFL would never have been realized.

What kind of coach are you to your child? Your kid will run into plenty of "never" people in this life—but the word "never," when it comes to your kid's dreams, represents the devil. Don't be a "never" person. Be God's advocate for your kid.

As the family coach, guide your child. Believe in his dreams. Pray together, sweat together, be your child's best coach, cheerleader, and advocate—and then ask God to help your child live out his dream wisely.

"The things which are impossible with men are possible with God" (Luke 18:27).

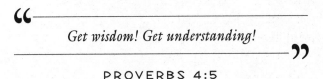

CHAPTER FOUR

BE WISE

> *Get wisdom! Get understanding!*

PROVERBS 4:5

The value of a young mind is inestimable.

When a mad scientist named John set out to build a human, he visited a brain store to buy the perfect brain. Several models, each carefully extracted from a dying subject, floated in a physiologically correct solution, tastefully displayed in refrigerated glass cases.

Three prominently displayed brains drew John's attention. These prime candidates were large, with good texture, and had once been housed in the craniums of successful professionals.

The first brain came from a forty-year-old lawyer known for his persuasiveness, compassion, and honesty. The price tag: one million dollars. The placard on the next brain described a five-star general who commanded thousands of men and was highly regarded for his courage and leadership. Also one million dollars. The third million-dollar specimen belonged to a well-known female neurosurgeon, whose own brain cells harbored intriguing information about the human brain.

Discouraged by the high prices, John continued his search, looking for something a little more affordable for his experiment. As he browsed through the glass cases, he saw a smaller brain back in a corner. It looked healthy and well-preserved, so he inquired about its availability.

That brain, the manager informed him, came from a ten-year-old boy who died in a skateboarding accident.

"How much?" John asked.

"Look," the manager told him, "why don't you consider one of those other three? They really are an excellent deal."

"How much?" John insisted.

"Ten million."

UNTAPPED POTENTIAL

WISE GUYS

Young brains are small. Seen from the grand stretch of a lifetime, they have barely been used. But don't look down on a child's lack of brain content. Adult brains, while hopefully full of knowledge, are fully grown and their potential somewhat maximized. In many ways, they are what they are. The child's brain, however, is more capable of learning. A child's potential remains largely untapped.

Did you know that a mature adult brain weighs about two and a half to three pounds and consists of 10 billion cells? Nerve impulses in an adult travel at three to four hundred feet per second. Once damaged, most nerves can't regenerate.

By contrast, an infant's brain grows at an incredible rate: 1,000 times faster than a fifteen-year-old, and 100,000 times faster than a fifty-year-old. You can figure out that the fifteen-year-old brain grows 100 times faster than the fifty-year-old brain. (You might not want to share that bit of trivia with your teenager.) Up through young adulthood, the brain of a child consists of billions of developing neurons and synapses. They are like a road map waiting to be filled in with thousands of miles of uncharted highways and channels.

Now do you see why a child's brain is priceless? The untapped potential of a child's mind is enormous! If we invest in young minds now, the returns will be immeasurable.

Cramming our kids with knowledge isn't the answer. Knowledge, the accumulation of facts and information, is incomplete—and, on its own, even dangerous.

Knowledge can make a person appear educated. But *wisdom* grants the ability to use knowledge correctly. We can feed our young people hours of statistics, facts, theories, and ideas, but without wisdom, their brains become mere storage houses, lacking in skills for creativity, problem-solving, and decision-making.

That's why the writer of Proverbs exclaimed so passionately, "Get wisdom!" Our young people already act like wise guys most of the time. Our job is to impart to them true wisdom, helping them become truly wise.

PREPARATION

NO WASTED MINDS

The United Negro College Fund coined the phrase "A mind is a terrible thing to waste." Minds are wasted when as a society (1) we don't acknowledge the great potential of young minds, and (2) we lose patience with the process that must occur for the healthy development of young minds.

Most people who watch TV sports are unaware of the intense mental preparation that goes on before each game.

During an average week in the NFL, we spent nine hours on the field practicing for a three-hour game. What goes unnoticed is the twelve to eighteen hours spent in the classroom. We watched films, memorized strategies, and even took two or three written exams per week, some about nine pages long. We spent far more time studying our opponents than we did playing against them.

The coaches spent sixteen-hour days in the office scheming plays to outthink the opponent. The night before the game, some slept at the stadium to keep focused. As physical as football is, the mental aspect of the game is more important. Without wisdom to make the right decisions, the game is lost.

The analogy to our kids' lives is obvious. Winning at life takes time, preparation, training, knowledge, and patience—the building blocks of wisdom. Because we are an instant gratification society, we try to leap over the sweaty stuff and go for the instant win. It doesn't work in football, and it certainly doesn't work that way in life. When we bypass the process, our kids are the losers. When society or parents—even the church—dangles the lie of instant success, disillusionment lurks right around the corner, waiting to destroy our kids' future.

Wisdom waits for the process.

THE WHOLE GAME

WHAT ABOUT NOW?

If getting wisdom takes time, what about now? What about kids who are wrecking their lives in the time it takes to read this book, much less try to teach them some smarts? They need wisdom, and they need it now. They can't wait!

Here's the good news: You have a God who works in the immediate *and* over the long haul. Listen to God's Word in James 1:5: "If any of you lacks wisdom, let him ask of God, who gives to all liberally and without reproach, and it will be given to him."

Look at your kid and think about that. With that verse in hand, you know you can come to God and ask for wisdom for yourself and your kids—and He will answer. The first thing you can do is start praying today for wisdom for your child.

But you also need to put the Scripture in context. It's no accident that the three verses preceding it go like this: "Consider it pure joy, my brothers, whenever you face trials of many kinds, because you know that the testing of your faith develops perseverance. Perseverance must finish its work so that you may be mature and complete" (NIV).

Wisdom can be compared to salvation, God's process of saving those who believe in Him. While God gives you the gift of eternal life the instant you accept His forgiveness and invite Jesus to rule your life, He also has a plan for maturing you by faith. He allows time to "work out your own salvation with fear and trembling, for it is God who works in you . . ." (Philippians 2:12–13).

You ask for wisdom, God grants it. But He develops wisdom in you through the process of trial and response, hard stuff and perseverance. That's a message to communicate to your kids. Prepare them mentally for the whole game, not just a few plays.

SOUND DECISIONS
WHAT WOULD YOUR CHILD DO?

Imagine you had the ability to grant your child whatever he or she desires—travel, material goods, fun, power, influence, or anything else.

As a young man, Solomon was on the receiving end of such a deal. He already led a privileged life as King David's son. When he inherited the throne of Israel upon David's death, he suddenly faced enormous responsibilities.

The Lord appeared to Solomon one night in a dream and said, "Ask! What shall I give you?" (1 Kings 3:5). Anything! God says, in effect, "Tell me what you want and I'll grant it."

Solomon didn't ask for riches or long life, or to have his enemies destroyed. He asked for an understanding heart and the ability to discern good and evil. He asked for wisdom.

A parent's dream come true! A young man who asks for wisdom when he could have called for beer and a big-screen TV! But look at the reasons he gives for this request: "You have shown great mercy to your servant David my father," Solomon said to the Lord, "because he walked before You in truth, in righteousness, and in uprightness of heart with You . . ." (3:6).

The example was set by his father. David, by no means a perfect man, nevertheless taught his son this great truth: "The fear of the Lord is the beginning of wisdom" (Psalm 111:10). Solomon grew up knowing that wisdom begins with respect for and knowledge of God. He eventually wrote that statement (Proverbs 9:10) and filled the book of Proverbs with other wise sayings. He had so much wisdom that world leaders came to listen to him. He taught about birds, fish, and plants. His wisdom helped him develop great wealth and military power, as well as make judicious decisions. Wisdom guided his building of the temple of God.

As long as Solomon used this wonderful gift, his life was blessed. You can read his legacy of wisdom in the Bible book of Proverbs. You can also read in the book of Ecclesiastes how he strayed from his wise ways and found nothing but emptiness and despair. His honest, personal account makes us understand why he wrote with such passion, "Get wisdom!" I believe he would add, "And hang onto it!"

Your kids need wisdom to discern good from evil, to avoid dangerous situations, to make sound decisions concerning education, drugs, sex, career, marriage—everything. Just as David inspired Solomon, parents need practical ways to help kids desire wisdom.

VALUE OF KNOWLEDGE

PARENTS AND PIT SCHOOLS

One of the most evil and effective weapons used against slaves in America was preventing them from learning to read or write. If a slave was caught reading, his finger was cut off. Slave owners knew that education brought liberation. Strong muscles led to productivity in the fields. Strong minds led to autonomy in the world.

Realizing this, a courageous group of slaves risked everything— lives included—to learn to read and write and to teach their children. They started "pit schools." Deep in the forest, slaves dug holes in the ground so they could meet at night without being seen. They sat down in the dirt and taught one another by dim candlelight. They knew the only escape from bondage was to be independent of mind. Their masters signed all their papers and made all their decisions. They weren't treated as thinking human beings.

The pit schools changed all that.

Learning increased the quality of the slaves' lives and gave them hope for a better tomorrow. But the real brilliance of the pit schools was the fact that they were created in the first place. Someone came to the conclusion that slaves would get nowhere without an education. The concept spread as those willing to pay the price made education possible.

That was wisdom at work. People decided they needed something, then took the steps necessary to get it. As a parent, you have the privilege of establishing or continuing that legacy in your family. No one else will ever sign your name or make your decisions or dictate your beliefs, as long as you have the wisdom to use your brain.

Sonya Carson grew up with little wisdom to influence her decisions. Because she had a heart condition, she was told she couldn't attend school. Case workers shuffled her from foster home to foster home throughout childhood. Certainly no one thought of her as wise.

She wasn't wise when, at age thirteen, she married a man who already had five kids and a wife. She wasn't wise when she tried to kill herself after her two sons were born and her husband left her. Her life was riddled with unwise choices until the day she got a call from her son's school. Big trouble. He had tried to stab another student.

Now Sonya became wise—wise enough to learn from her own life and to want better for her sons. After assessing her situation, she decided her sons would go nowhere stabbing instead of studying.

She made some hard decisions and enforced them. She limited her boys to two television shows per week. She made them read, then explain to her and to each other what they read. She had them read the book of Proverbs to her from the Bible. It became her favorite book. She pushed them, made them study, directed them toward quality materials, and helped them take full advantage of their intellectual potential.

Today, Sonya's older son, Curtis Carson, is an engineer. Her younger son, Dr. Ben Carson, is the world-renowned director of pediatric neurosurgery at Johns Hopkins Hospital. Sonya Carson's sacrifice and wisdom helped her make decisions that changed her sons' lives. That wisdom, passed down to her sons, guides them even now.

Sonya learned from her own life. She saw what was lacking. Just like the parents in the slave days who risked everything for the pit schools, mothers like Sonya Carson are willing to do what it takes to help their children make better lives.

All of us need to ask ourselves if we are doing everything possible to teach wisdom to our kids:

Are we setting an example? Are we willing to sacrifice to create opportunities for our children? Would we go to the lengths those parents did who created the pit schools? Are we willing to challenge our children the way Sonya Carson did—and follow through with it?

CHALLENGE THEM
KIDS DON'T WANT TO BE STUPID

One night I dropped by a local ice rink to check on some kids from our neighborhood who were having a party. I heard a fight might break out between rival Filipino gangs and wanted to prevent trouble. They're just a bunch of little guys from our block, I figured, no big deal.

It was a big deal—a potential shoot-out between an L.A. gang and a San Diego Samoan gang. The first guy I ran into stood 6'9". His head was as big as my chest. I knew he was big because the cigarette in his mouth looked like a piece of lint on his lip.

I was trying to figure out how to exit without looking like a cowardly punk, when a fight broke out in the room where Goliath stood. I saw a little guy—who would be David in this story—yanked out of the room. Someone was trying to save his life. I followed him around for a while, then finally approached him to tell him I was keeping an eye out for him. I told him someone else was watching out for him too.

"Who?" he asked suspiciously.

I told him Jesus was following him. Well, he started cursing and yelling at me, and turned to walk away. Then I asked him if he was stupid.

That got him really mad. I asked him again, "Are you stupid?"

He said no. Then I asked, "If I offered you one million dollars for free would you take it?" He was suspicious and wouldn't answer. I took the direct approach. I told him that if he didn't ask Jesus to be his Savior, he would go to hell. But if he would admit that Jesus is Lord and believe that God raised Jesus from the dead, he would be saved. I challenged him to make a decision about his life.

All this was taking place in one very cold ice rink, so I was praying he'd make some kind of decision soon. He took his time, but that night he prayed to become a Christian. I found out he was part of a notorious Detroit street gang, ironically called the Disciples.

What provoked that encounter? A resistance to being called stupid. Kids don't want to look dumb. They don't want to be unwise. They avoid situations that reveal their ignorance and gravitate toward places that make them feel intellectually at ease. It's no accident that young people who do poorly in school are prone to experimenting with drugs, sex, and alcohol. Lacking wisdom and self-confidence, they seek to hide their inadequacies.

I know it sounds like I really got in this kid's face and forced a decision. But I also know kids need to be challenged to be wise.

TAKE A CHANCE

THE SCHOLARS

Aaron was barely eleven when a man in a suit and tie came to his classroom. He was looking for fifty students from Aaron's south-central Los Angeles school to accept a challenge. If they could meet his conditions, the prize was an $80,000 four-year scholarship to the University of Southern California.

Fifty students were interviewed and selected, all minority kids from the turbulent streets surrounding the school. They were average students, pulling mostly C's, sixth graders reading at a third-grade level. Under their current circumstances, the chance that any of these kids would make it to college—much less to USC, the "rich man's school"—was practically zero.

Mr. James Fleming deliberately offered his challenge to mediocre students. "Everyone's after the cream of the crop," he said. "Give me the average Joe or Joan who can grasp 70 to 75 percent of what goes on in the class, and I can teach them to love learning."

The fifty selected were called "scholars" and the program an academy. Aaron, a young man once called stupid by his third-grade teacher because he couldn't spell, made the cut. He recalls being told during his interview, "This isn't an entitlement program. Do you think you can keep up?" Aaron was scared and felt inadequate, but nevertheless answered, "Yes, I can."

The scholars attended early morning classes at USC, then spent the rest of the day at their regular schools. They returned to USC on Saturdays, on top of completing three hours of homework each night. The work load and rules—maintain higher grade levels, forgo the baggy pants and bare midriff look of their peers, and give up playtime for tutoring time—scared off several students the first two weeks.

Despite learning disabilities and family problems, Aaron hung in there. Like the other students, the enormous commitment brought his personal problems to a head. Weekly counseling was arranged for each scholar.

Fleming knew not all the students would make it to USC, but that, regardless, their lives would be radically altered. The program offered more than tuition money. The students learned survival skills and discipline and uncovered talents and potential they never knew they possessed. Aaron's C average rose to an A-minus. He scored over seven hundred on his SAT. And he developed a passion for writing.

Twice Aaron tried to quit but was talked out of it. Over the next several years, students dropped out for a variety of reasons, usually discipline related. Others were brought in as replacements, bringing the high school graduating class of scholars to forty-six. All but three applied to USC during their senior year.

Aaron nagged his mother every day to check the mail as he waited nervously for the envelope to arrive. Had he shot too high? He hadn't just applied for admission; he wanted to get into the engineering school.

Aaron, the third-grade boy who couldn't spell, finally received his acceptance into USC's engineering program. Sixteen of his peers had also made it to USC. Those who didn't have gone on to other colleges and career goals. None of them regrets that they were challenged to change their lives.

One last point to this story: When Aaron and his peers signed the contract to be admitted into Mr. Fleming's academic program, parents weren't allowed to stand on the sidelines and beam. They, too, signed a contract promising to uphold the rules and commitment. *Most of the students who failed to make it into USC were those whose parents did not uphold their end of the contract.* Parents, we, too, have a challenge to meet.

PLAY YOUR PART

THE PARENTS' JOB

Parents play an enormous part in developing a child's ability to make good choices in friends, activities, and intellectual pursuits. But sometimes we don't realize how vital our role is, nor do we know exactly what to do.

Pastor James Milford, quoted in Josh McDowell's book *Right From Wrong*, gave this impassioned plea to his church:

> Our children are not adopting our values and morals. They do not share our priorities. And we cannot blame the media, we cannot blame society, we cannot blame government, we cannot blame the Supreme Court—they are not entrusted with communicating biblical values to our children—we are.

We have not only failed to take charge of our children's education, we have failed to take part in it. How many of us have gotten to know our children's principals and teachers? How many school board meetings have we attended? When was the last time we volunteered to chaperone field trips? I'm afraid we have expected others to take primary responsibility for what our children know and what they value.

On a more secular note, in 1991 the National Commission on Children acknowledged that "Schools should encourage and facilitate parent participation in governance and management processes and in school activities." In other words, parents, you are needed. You are indispensable to your children's education. You can't be a spectator.

When our son was born, my wife was in labor for forty-nine hours. At hour forty-four his head got stuck. The next five hours were, as you can imagine, grueling. My wife had an attitude by the time our boy was born.

His head was huge! The average infant's head makes up 30 percent of birth weight. My son's head tipped in at 40 percent. We feared he would either be funny-looking or nine feet tall by the time he grew into his head. I'm happy to report that he's growing up nicely proportioned, and we keep telling him that his head is so big because of all the brains in it. We also tell him he's accountable to use those brains.

Look at your child. Put your hand on his or her head and for a moment think of all the potential inside there. The ability to learn, reason, and comprehend things you and I may never know about. Your child has been uniquely gifted. What is he doing about it? More importantly, how are *you* helping your child along? Here are some suggestions to get you started:

1. REVIEW YOUR CHILD'S SCHOOL PROGRESS WEEKLY

Get to know in detail how your child is doing in school. Parents, you are your kids' best teacher. Take a few minutes each day to review homework, test grades, papers. Ask for weekly progress reports to be sent home, a common practice in many classrooms. Don't wait for report cards to come out and find out too late that little Jenny is failing math and is now too far behind to ever catch up. Stay on top of your kids' grades.

2. MAKE SURE YOUR KIDS READ

God chose the written Word to reveal himself to us. He ordained the written word as a powerful tool for communication. The ability to read will give your child access to truth, wisdom, and knowledge. Make it a priority to know your child's reading level. If your child falls behind, find out what you can do to help. Some schools have reading specialists. You may have to hire a tutor. You can read with your child every night—then have her read back to you. Start with a few Bible verses, or pick a favorite book that becomes a project you read together.

Students with strong reading skills do better in both school and career. While every student won't read at the same level, only you can make sure your child achieves the highest level she can.

3. DISCOVER YOUR CHILD'S STRENGTHS AND WEAKNESSES

Do you know what your child is good at? Do you know which subjects are difficult? Tuning in to your child's strengths and weaknesses will give you an idea of his gifts and talents and what activities and careers he should pursue. The process of discovering this information will deepen your relationship and help you guide your son or daughter to set goals and work toward them.

4. ALLOW YOUR CHILD TO TEACH YOU

One day my daughter saw a newspaper article about a twelve-year-old boy who committed suicide. When she asked what it all meant, I knew it was time to discuss a difficult subject with her. I told her to read the article and tell me about it. She was heartbroken, curious, indignant—so many emotions ran through her as she excitedly told me about the story.

Soon I noticed her reading other articles. She began to take an interest in reading and sharing what she read. She knew she had an interested party to listen.

When I work with kids at church and Bible study, I do the same thing. They ask me a question, and I turn it around by giving them a general idea where to look something up in the Bible. I ask them to research the passage, read it, and tell everyone else what it means. They gleam when they discover concepts themselves and actually have the opportunity to share them. It's better to teach people to fish than to hand them fish already caught.

5. USE THE "SO WHAT?" FACTOR

Teenage Julie chattered away at the dinner table, reciting facts and statistics about a controversial social issue. She came home armed with this knowledge from her high school social studies class. When she stopped to take a breath, her dad quietly asked, "What does all this mean?"

"What do you mean, 'what does it mean?' " she responded.

"Well," Dad said, "tell me what this means to you. How does it affect our family and our society?"

Julie thought a moment, then ventured forth a couple of opinions, which launched a lively family discussion of the issue.

What a wise father. He challenged his daughter to think about what she knew and what it meant. I call this the "So What?" factor. You can challenge your kids to press for real-life application in schoolwork, Bible study, and news stories. Rather than merely assimilate information, they can practice processing, to think about a subject and ask questions.

6. LEARN TO USE KNOWLEDGE CORRECTLY

I also tell my kids to be selective about what they need to know and to toss out what clutters up their minds. My daughter was studying for a huge California history test. She wasn't doing well because she wasn't comprehending what she was reading.

So we tackled the problem with a highlighter pen—a small technique but new to her. We told her to read and mark what she thought was important. To look at what was emphasized, italicized, and what the teacher talked about in class. To be selective about what she memorized because she couldn't memorize every word. My daughter needed to wisely use information to her advantage.

Obviously this isn't an original study plan. But when it worked beautifully to bring up my daughter's grade, I told her to take that lesson with her whenever she processed information. Her brain is bombarded with millions of pieces of knowledge daily. To be wise, she needs to sift every thought, idea, or concept she takes in—and train her mind to highlight and remember, or toss away as unedifying and unnecessary.

How can she best filter? Each of us can start by asking God. The beginning of wisdom is fear of the Lord, I remind kids. God's Holy Spirit will be your Sifter. He asks us to bring "every thought into captivity to the obedience of Christ" (2 Corinthians 10:5). I pray each day for God to show my kids what they need to know and how to use it, and to protect their minds from the garbage that society throws at them.

7. IMPLEMENT THE WISE-UP METER

All parents fear their children won't possess the wisdom to make wise choices. Whether you live in the suburbs, country, or city, your children need to make crucial decisions every day.

The search for wisdom isn't as far-flung as it might seem. The Bible says wisdom cries out from the street. The principles of wisdom are all around us if we will only listen. So, using some already established concepts, I developed the "Wise-Up Meter" to use with my youth groups and my own kids—and to give parents a tool for teaching their children to assess a situation.

1. Objectively *define the problem.* Jot it down. Try to be une-

motional and nonjudgmental at this point. Just define the issue. For example, write down "Getting High."

2. Discuss the *benefits* of being involved in this activity. Have the young person actually list reasons, such as these hypothetical ones: (a) it's fun; (b) my friends all do it; (c) it helps me relax.

3. Now list the *dangers* of being involved: (a) harmful to health; (b) illegal; (c) dangerous while driving.

4. Discuss *problem-solving steps* they can take to avoid getting involved: (a) change my friends; (b) get counseling; (c) get involved in sports or other activities; (d) prayer.

This is a simple outline, a short example. In reality, if you take the time to really discuss the issue and urge a young person to draw from television programs, magazine articles, music, friends' lives, and other research sources, you will be surprised at how eagerly they might attack an issue. In time this will become a thought process your kids will learn to use on their own.

You'll think of multiple topics on your own, but for starters look for opportunities—the earlier the better—to deal with the following issues:

peer pressure

picking friends

how to avoid being tempted by
    drugs

how to be treated like a lady

how to act like a gentleman

sexually transmitted diseases

sexual behavior

gangs

homosexuality

anorexia and bulimia

moral issues in the news

suicide

cheating and lying

greed

wise dating

abortion

career dreams

marriage

whatever you know is
    important.

Consider keeping a list to record issues you have discussed with your son or daughter and issues that remain. Your list will remind you to pray and to be ready when God opens the door to discussion.

Don't put off discussing difficult subjects with your child because you feel ill equipped. You might have to do your homework, but God offers you wisdom. And to keep the discussion fair to everyone, give you and your child the right to say, "I don't know," and go looking for more data.

I didn't specifically list God or faith because God's Word should be your primary source of wisdom in teaching your kids. Your child's relationship with the Lord isn't just another issue on the list. It lays the foundation for everything else.

8. PRESENT "WHAT IF..." SCENARIOS

The key to using any of these teaching tools is time. Take time to sit and talk with your children, to strategize, teach, and listen to what they think and know.

I like "what if..." scenarios. I sit and talk with kids and throw out lines like "What if you found yourself alone in a car with a boy you really like and he starts making moves on you?" After a few giggles and blushes, you'll find out what that young girl knows, and you might be amazed at what she *doesn't* know that she *should* know to protect herself.

Once you have raised the subject and discovered what they don't know, ask them to research it, think about it, or search the Bible for answers—whatever is appropriate for the issue—and then talk to you about it again. Knowing what to do ahead of time in a variety of situations will increase your child's ability to make wise decisions.

What if...

you need to call 9-1-1?
you need to cook your own dinner?
there's a fire in the house?
you're at a party where other kids start drinking,
      including your ride home?
someone needs CPR?
you need to admit yourself to a hospital?
you have a friend you suspect is anorexic (or addicted to

drugs, nicotine, alcohol, etc.)?

you have to wash your own clothes?

your car breaks down out in the middle of nowhere or at night?

your little brother or sister starts bleeding?

you're out someplace and someone starts shooting?

you need to find a job?

someone you know is talking about suicide?

your boyfriend (or girlfriend) wants to have sex?

Kids are faced with these issues—and more—every day. Wise choices don't often result from on-the-spot reactions. Give them an opportunity to think in advance about what they would do.

9. WATCH, READ, AND DISCUSS THE NEWS TOGETHER

Kids are going to hear what's going on in the world. Processing the news together will help them make sense of what they hear and learn from it. Use the following list as a starting point for working with your kids:

Use news to teach vocabulary—like DNA, mistrial, defense attorney, independent counsel, plea bargain, death sentence, peace treaty. As long as there is news, there will be new words in your child's life.

Use news to acquaint your kids with geography. Keep a world globe or map near the TV. Help your child find places like Bosnia, Baghdad, and Afghanistan.

Discuss the issues. Why is there conflict between North and South Korea? Why is there racial tension in South Africa? Why are Jews and Palestinians always fighting? What are the differences between kings, queens, prime ministers, and presidents?

Use news to explain how current events relate to the Bible, historically and/or prophetically.

Assign a story to a child and ask him or her to track it for a week. You'll be surprised at how eagerly that young person will open the paper, find the story, and give you the daily update.

Use the Internet, magazines, and special journals. Spending just ten minutes a day to discover and discuss the news with your children will help them learn to put information in its proper place, discern its relevance to their world, and use it correctly—which is the real application of wisdom.

10. INVOLVE YOUR KIDS IN FAMILY PLANS

The Robinson family faced a sudden loss in income. The dad had been working two jobs to cover their expenses and to allow his wife to stay home with their four children. When he lost his second job, Mr. Robinson called a family meeting. After praying for wisdom and guidance, they held a brainstorming session to come up with creative ways to save and make money. They planned garage sales, babysitting jobs, lemonade stands. They agreed to cut back cable TV service, turn off lights more diligently, cut coupons, give up certain activities and hot lunches at school.

They made it through the lean time, and the kids learned valuable lessons about planning, budgeting, working as a team, sacrifice, faith, and the wise use of money.

As they become old enough, bring your kids in on family issues. Let them help plan vacations, meals, and activities. Discuss decisions such as buying a car or moving or getting a family pet. Let them learn to pray about and think through important issues. It's great practical training for the future.

11. PROMOTE WISE CAREER PLANNING

Young people get jazzed about pursuing a specific career or college major. Without discouraging them, ask them what they *really* know about their choice—and then help them find out more. The Bible says zeal without knowledge is not a good thing.

Asking hard questions will help them decide if this is something they really want or if it's just a cool thing to talk about. Again, tell them to do their research, starting with the following questions:

What do you want to do?

Why?

Do you know anyone already doing this?

What do you need to do to get started?

What are the benefits?

What are the dangers?

How will you overcome or deal with the dangers?

Have you seen others fail? Why did they fail?

What training or education is required and how long will it take?

Is this something you see yourself doing five years from now? Ten? Twenty?

There are many more things you can discuss, but the point is to make young people think and count the cost of their choices. The thought process involved will get them moving. As pastor Stuart Briscoe says, you can't steer a parked car. As you pray for your child, you can trust the Lord to steer left or right, according to His will.

You're probably thinking that this pursuit of wisdom will take a lot of time. You're right. It requires time to talk with and listen to your child. You are in the process of developing him into a thinker and a savvy adult able to pursue goals wisely. All of us are busy people, but developing wisdom in your child is worth more than all your other business. "The greatest good is wisdom," wrote St. Augustine. Teach your child the greatest good.

You can pay attention in the beginning, or pay the price later. Now there's a good discussion question: Which do you think is the wisest choice?

GOOD THINGS

DESTINED TO BE WISE

The traits we pray to see in our kids don't develop overnight. As adults, we are still growing in Christ. We can expect no more from our kids. But I also don't believe God wants us to expect any less than His best for our children. He has destined His children to be wise.

Take heart, and reread James 1:5. When you ask for wisdom for yourself and for your children, you have a mighty and awesome God who wants to bestow gifts on His children, and wisdom is truly one of His greatest gifts.

"What man is there among you," Jesus asks in Matthew 7:9–11, *"who, if his son asks for bread, will give him a stone? Or if he asks for a fish, will he give him a serpent? If you then, being evil, know how to give good gifts to your children, how much more will your Father who is in heaven give good things to those who ask Him!"*

CHAPTER FIVE

DESTINED TO...
BE WORTHY

> "
> *I am fearfully and wonderfully made.*
> "
>
> PSALM 139:14

November 11, 1985, was a Sunday, and the due date for our first child. It was also the day of one of my biggest games of the year, a showdown with our arch rival, the Los Angeles Raiders.

My head wasn't exactly in the game. All I could think about was my wife and the little girl I was hoping for.

The game went into the first overtime of my four-year NFL career. I ran to the locker room and heard, "Miles, get to the hospital." I showered before the rest of the team got off the field, nearly hit some fans in the crowded parking lot, and arrived at the hospital just in time to watch the birth of my baby girl. She had a cone head and funny spots all over her face, but I had the same reaction every parent has: My baby was the most beautiful sight I had ever seen.

What I didn't anticipate in my response to this miracle of life was the surge of self-sacrificing love I suddenly felt within me. I realized afresh how God, my heavenly Father, loves me unconditionally. His love burned in my heart for my daughter, a love I was now entrusted to reflect into her life. I committed that day to do whatever it took to make my little girl happy.

We were so careful with her—gentle in how we held her, fed her, talked to her. Every new stage of her life was exciting as we watched her grow and learn to walk and talk. We wanted so badly for her to succeed. We counted her a beautiful gift from God.

Still one thing troubled me. Clearly my wife and I knew she was precious. Even you might be able to look through my eyes and appreciate my daughter. But the question in my mind was this: Would *she* think that way? Would she know that she is a priceless gift and a child of God? Would she understand how much she is loved?

I want her to know her "worthability."

WORTHABILITY

HOW CHILDREN SEE THEMSELVES

Throughout this book I invite you, the parent, to change your viewpoint—to see your child as God sees him or her. I want you to look at your son or daughter with hope, especially if you have struggled with worry or anxiety.

In this chapter, however, I want to talk about how children see themselves. They will have achieved one of life's highest—and most difficult—tasks when they can look in a mirror, see themselves as God's creation, and be proud of what He made.

I want our children to be confident that God made no mistakes when He created them. They are "His workmanship" (Ephesians 2:10). He created them with good thoughts and good plans, not to harm them but to give them "a future and a hope" (Jeremiah 29:11). They need to believe that their positive points—as well as things in themselves they see as negative—are part of His plan. In God, they have worth and identity. In God, they have ability. They need a clear belief that as God's creation they are something special. It's what I call "worthability."

FAMILY LIFE

A BURDENED GENERATION

I strongly believe a child's worthability quotient is profoundly raised or lowered by the quality of his or her family life.

And yet we have to answer this: If a child's worthability and self-respect are so rooted in strong family and faith values, why do kids from good homes still struggle? I see it all the time. I study parents and how they run a family, then I watch the kids and it doesn't compute. Of course, I deal with a lot of kids whose lack of worthability is pretty understandable. Their home lives are a mess. Nothing at home reinforces their personal value. But what about the apparently good homes?

I began to realize that today's children are beaten down. They carry not only their own problems but those of the world as well. They can't wiggle free from the weight, because an all-pervasive media keeps us informed about anything and everything. The headlines this morning, for example, offered plenty for sensitive kids and teens to worry about—nuclear bomb detonations in India and Pakistan, bloody student riots in Indonesia, and smoke from Mexican brush fires drifting across the southern U.S. and forcing school children to stay indoors. This media assault makes kids both apathetic and hedonistic. Their hope erodes when such constant tragedy pours over them, so they develop an "eat, drink, and be merry, for tomorrow you die" approach to living.

Ironically, the generation having such a hard time growing up also carries too many adult burdens.

Most of today's young adults and children have been parented by children of the '60s, who, growing up, had material wealth but often lacked security, roots, and godly values. While '60s kids attempted to regain lost ground as they matured to adulthood, they brought questions, insecurities, and problems into parenting today's children. Children and teens today carry the emotional burdens of their families because their parents are still trying to get it together.

Asking kids to bear the burden of adult issues or emotions is a load that makes kids feel inadequate. It weighs down their worthability. So think through the following points. Ask yourself if any of the things described apply to how you relate to your kids. Check out these worthability-crushing messages parents unintentionally communicate:

1. If parents make a child responsible for meeting adult needs, they're telling the child, "You're not valuable as a child." I know young people who regularly counsel their parents. Because of their own shattered or displaced families, the parents lack a strong support system, so they lean on their kids to meet their needs. It's almost as if they had children to replace the family they lost growing up.

Kids shouldn't feel responsible for the personal lives of their parents. They need to be able to look at their mom and dad and find security and stability. Unfortunately, young people end up feeling obligated to supply what their parents lack. Ask yourself if you ever depend on your children to fulfill any of the following needs:

companionship and love

success in school, sports, or career

emotional stability

empathy and insight for dealing with adult problems

recognition for beauty or good looks

popularity

Most of us have seen obnoxious Little League fathers playing out Major League fantasies through their sons or daughters. But look for subtle ways you live through your child. Be proud of your kids, but also take time to pray and ask yourself why you want to be proud—for their sake or for yours?

2. If parents fear what their adult peers think about their parenting, they're telling the child, "You embarrass me." You expect a baby to spit up and spoil your suit as you head off to work or church. But babies can't make you look all that bad. Bigger kids—that's another story. Your unease grows with your child.

He screams and hits you when you say no to him in a store.

She heads out the door in a dirty, mismatched outfit.

He forgets to brush his teeth before school.

She doesn't get the grades the neighbor kids do.

He shows up high at a junior high dance and gets brought home in a squad car.

She zooms off with a tattooed biker as all your neighbors look on.

He lands on the front page of the newspaper—and not for civic responsibility.

Honesty requires us to admit that we fear the reactions of both friends and strangers to these events almost as much as we feel concern for our child.

Make it your goal to shut out what your peers think. And slow down so that your words and actions at home aren't determined by your wounded pride but by what would best help your wayward child.

3. If parents treat a young person like a miniature adult, they're telling the child, "You're not as capable as I thought." Rather than realizing that teenagers are in many ways children, we expect them to act like adults in pint-sized packages. We assume they can navigate the world, make wise decisions, and use good judgment. When they fail—and they will because they're both human *and* still kids—our disappointment becomes a heavy burden for them to carry.

At a Q and A session during a parent/teen conference, one teenager wrote on his question card, "What do I do if my parents think I am flawless and should never make mistakes? Every time I mess up they act as if this is never supposed to happen."

No kid deserves to be punished just for being a kid. Your young person needs supervision, instruction, and guidance longer than you might think—or than she admits. When she makes mistakes, talk them through with her, show understanding, and help her get up to face the next bout in life. Love is often about learning through second chances (or third, fourth, etc.).

Most kids don't begin exhibiting adult behavior until their late teens or early twenties—and that's if they are fortunate enough to have a strong, stable sense of worthability and value. Most young adults are still trying to figure life out. They need room for making immature, young adult decisions. Allowing them independence in increasingly large areas over many years keeps them from making their first big choices big mistakes.

4. If parents force a child to fend for himself, they're telling the child, "You're not worth my time." I hear it all the time: "I feel alone even in a crowd." Lack of consistent, affirming communication between adult role models and children makes for a lonely childhood. The teenagers I talk to confess that they feel isolated— then go on to painfully describe parents too busy launching second careers, moving out of the house because of separation or divorce, or suffering a mid-life crisis.

Fear of facing the world solo is often what brings feelings of loneliness and worthlessness to a head. Young people make more choices and changes during their teens and early twenties than they will make for the rest of their lives. They need us as sounding boards. They need us to teach them how to make decisions without telling them what to do. They need us to remember some of the pain of early adulthood. Kids who have high worthability are the ones who have someone taking a personal interest in them—sometimes parents, sometimes mentors and disciplers.

DISCERN REALITY

LOOKS GOOD ON THE OUTSIDE ... BUT

Churches and schools can easily be fooled by kids' apparent outward moral conformity. Or by their poise with parents, teachers, and other adults. I've known countless Christian kids who have grown up in the church and Christian schools, learning along the way the right moves to play the part of a nice Christian boy or girl—and the right lines to mouth. But deep down inside, they're lost and confused.

I don't say this to scare or grieve parents. But we need to look past externals and discern reality so we can help our kids develop true worth, identity, and ability. After all, God is far more interested in developing deep, inner maturity than buffing us up to a surface shine. God doesn't polish rusty people. He rebuilds them.

When a kid's dress, talk, and actions are calculated solely to please adults, that kid splits into two people. On the surface are parts that please others. Buried is that part where flesh and spirit battle. Kids need the freedom to acknowledge that often it's hard to choose to do what's right. They have to find out God forgives them when they come clean. Kids who don't know God's forgiveness and empowerment will always struggle with worthability. They know they aren't right on the inside.

I AM WITH YOU

WHO AM I? I COULD NEVER DO THAT

Moses was busy herding his flock back across the desert when God talked to him from a burning bush and told him to go to Egypt and negotiate his people's freedom. Now, Moses was a convicted murderer in Egypt, and he had no plans to return to the scene of the crime. But the imprisonment of his people, the Israelites, shook him. And now God himself was tapping him as the man to set things right.

Moses must have been used to talking to God. If I were standing out in the desert and a burning bush started yammering at me, I don't think I'd say much back. But Moses recovered from the shock and responded to God's instructions with: "Who am I?" He had to know, *Who am I to do such a great thing? Why pick me?* He was thinking, *I'm not capable! I'm not worthy!*

That's what kids ask themselves every day. *Who am I? What makes me worth the space I take up on planet earth? Why think I can do anything great with my life—especially after the way I've messed up?*

God gave Moses the same answer He gives to each of us and to our kids: "I will certainly be with you." What does this have to do with Moses' self-doubts? Everything! God was saying, "You're the man." Why? "Because I'm with you." God let Moses know that his worthability wasn't defined by what others thought of him or what he could accomplish on his own but by whom he belonged to.

God was saying to Moses as He says to us, "You belong to Me. My ownership of you gives you worthability and importance. You have value because you are made in My image, saved through My Son, filled by My Spirit." And God's "I will certainly be with you" made it possible for Moses to fulfill God's call.

Likewise, you can say to your kids, "Your worth isn't based on who you know. It isn't defined by your accomplishments or your looks or your past. Your worth isn't defined by *who* you are but by *whose* you are."

YOUTH IN ACTION

BEYOND THE BURNING BUSH

Teens might think of Moses as an old guy—the grizzly Ten Commandments dude. So let me tell you about the worthability of a young man and a young woman whose pride in their God-given identity gave them courage to risk death.

When the Babylonians raided Jerusalem around 605 B.C., the advancing armies were instructed by the king to spare talented, healthy *young* men. Daniel was one of those selected. The cunning plan was to train Daniel in the ways of Babylon, demand that he forsake his Jewish heritage, and groom him for political service in the Babylonian empire.

Daniel was a desirable choice because of his integrity and obvious worthiness. Unfortunately for the Babylonians, integrity came from a healthy sense of who he was. Daniel had no intention of losing his identity. He "purposed in his heart that he would not defile himself" (Daniel 1:8). Daniel refused to allow the Babylonians to change his name. He refused to allow the memory of his culture, family, and heritage to be erased. He refused to eat the king's diet, and, most of all, he refused to forsake his God.

Why? Daniel had a strong sense of his God-given worthability.

He knew he was special because God created him that way. He understood his purpose. So he was unconcerned about what people thought—or what they might threaten. In the culmination of Daniel's story, he refused to abandon his allegiance to the one true God and as a consequence was tossed into a den of lions. He was willing to stand up to the king to honor his worthability.

Had they hung out in the same time and place, Daniel would have seen in Esther a woman of similar heart. Chosen as a very young woman to be queen to the Persian king Ahasuerus, Esther one day found the fate of her entire people in her hands. Dazzled by her beauty, the king had no idea of her roots. When he sanctioned an order that all Jews in his land be exterminated, Esther the Jew had a choice to make. If she kept quiet, she could save her own life. If she stepped forward, she risked being killed herself along with her people.

Esther's roots in her faith and her culture were too deep to be denied. God had prepared her for this moment of pressure. With her strong identity in God and belief in His power in her life, she confronted the king, revealed her identity, and ultimately saved her race.

Esther's strong sense of accountability to her past gave her the strength to hold on to it when evil forces were threatening to take it away. Her upbringing provided her with belonging and affirmation and pride in her heritage. Her decision hinged on whether she would be who God made her or live in deception and become someone else.

An environment that nurtures a relationship with God and a family heritage gives children the security they need to thrive like Moses, Daniel, and Esther. A child raised in that spiritual richness will be apt to look boldly in the mirror, be proud of God's creation, and take joy in being the unique person God designed him or her to be.

ARE YOU DEVELOPING WORTHABILITY IN YOUR KIDS?

There are good ways you can increase the worthability factor in the life of your child.

Consider these questions as a gauge of how you are contributing to your child's worth:

1. Are you convinced that parenting is a process of equipping your child to leave you someday? Your kid is trying to figure out who he is and what he believes about life, himself, and his future. Remember, your child—particularly a teenage child—is steering through a winding transition. Detours on everything from friends and hairstyles to moods and music are normal in a process of discovering a personal road through life.

Worthability grows as a child develops individual ownership of his beliefs, not rotely accepting what you and other adults believe. God made your child to learn to think for himself. After all, you won't always be around to steer him. Some days you're already in the backseat as your kid heads for school, sports, and the rest of life. Later, when your kid is on his own, you're pretty much locked in the trunk.

One day a father took his daughter for a walk to watch the river near their house. The water was higher than usual and flowed rapidly. The little girl saw a pretty flower down the embankment close to the water. When she asked if she could pick it, her father said, "Yes, but don't let go of my hand." He let her go only as far as she could without letting go of his hand.

When your child is very young, she needs to hang on to you. But when she is ready to leave you, even to places where it appears dangerous and scary, are you able to let her go? That father's message—go ahead out into the world, but only as far as you can go while hanging on to me—is appropriate for a small child. But tight rules can't hold a child to your side forever. The only way to sanely and securely hold on to a grown child is through faith and prayer.

2. How does your child see herself when she looks through your eyes? Your child internalizes what you reflect to her. If the message you send through your words, actions, and attitudes is mistrust, disappointment, fear, worry, lack of confidence—those negative attitudes will slowly erode away your kid's worthability.

Pull out your yearbooks and remember what it was like to be fifteen, to want to be attractive and accepted. Communicate your own fears about growing up and your confidence that your son or daughter will grow up well-adjusted.

I saw a skit featuring two women playing a mother and a daughter. The daughter held a piece of paper in her hand that represented her self-image. Every time the parent questioned the daughter's worth, put the daughter down, or made the daughter feel unworthy of love, a piece of the paper was torn away and dropped to the floor. Even though on occasion the mother tried to do something positive or apologize for her negative input, the pieces of paper, once torn, could not be so easily attached again.

3. When you speak to your child, can you count more negative or positive words coming from your mouth? Psychologists contend it takes at least seven positive comments to undo one negative remark. Listen to what you say to your child. What do you hear? Look for positive, affirming, faith-building words: words spoken with respect in front of other adults and your child's peers; *thank you, I'm sorry,* and *please,* as often as you would want them said to you; words of affirmation and encouragement.

4. What motivates your parenting? The stress of child-raising can cause parents to rationalize a lot of behaviors. When you discipline your kid, make rules for his social life, and put up other boundaries and guidelines—what are your motives? Yes, you have to consider your sanity and your interests. But your bigger concern is finding ways to allow an independent young man or woman to develop. Children *need* rules that help them to be considerate of other people, so carefully pray about the balance. Make rules for their sake, not only yours.

A family I knew made 7:30–8:00 the absolute, no-exceptions bedtime in their household. Dad and Mom worked demanding jobs. They were dedicated parents, but by eight o'clock in the evening, they figured they needed time to themselves. That worked out okay while their son was young. But when they tried to enforce that bedtime hour into the junior high years—obviously not for their son's sake but for their own convenience—not surprisingly, he rebelled. Pretty soon he found ways to avoid coming home at night. They lost more sleep worrying about him than if they had set up reasonable guidelines to begin with.

5. Are you open and honest with your child, or do you avoid uncomfortable topics? If your child senses that some topics are out of bounds—so she feels blown off and her need for honest answers ignored—you are telling her she is (1) not important enough to know the truth, or (2) not capable of understanding either the truth or your need for privacy.

Your child learns communication skills from you. Don't let him think that the only way to handle an uncomfortable subject is avoidance. Being honest teaches honesty. Being straightforward teaches him to talk straight with you. If something is private, tell him so. Treat your child with enough respect to say something like, "Maybe someday you and I can discuss this. Right now, I need to keep it to myself because it's a very personal matter."

COMMITTED TO EXCELLENCE

GROWING YOUR KIDS' WORTHABILITY

Willie Jones was an A student, star wrestler, football player, and volunteer mentor. He was on his way to Cornell University to become a doctor. He was committed to excellence. When I met him, he held his head up, looked me in the eye, and didn't seem to feel the need to impress me or to be a phony. He wasn't arrogant but he was confident. His worthability ran deeper than even his talents and achievements. He was obviously proud of who God had made him to be and what God was going to do with his life. I felt like I wanted to see him again soon.

One day while watching the news, I heard Willie's name. I sat up and took notice as I heard the story tersely reported from an accident scene. While standing outside at a graduation party, Willie was accidentally shot and killed.

I attended his funeral, even though I didn't know him well. I wanted to pay my respects for all the talents God had given this young man, for the outstanding way he used them, for the way he had made the most of his short life. I couldn't get into the church! It was packed. Politicians, government officials, student athletes, family, friends—hundreds of people drawn there for the same reason I was. We were there to celebrate the life of someone who gave his all, did his best, reached for the top, and shared his passion with others. Willie knew he had worthability.

Frankly, I'd be a bit unnerved as a parent by such a "together" kid. It might be hard for me to let go and adjust to the fact that I'm not dealing with a child anymore—but looking eye-to-eye with a mature young man. But that's the worthability we want to see in our kids. We want them to know who they are and why they are here. We want them to love God, who made them, and to be happy with themselves.

Let's look at a few ways we can build worthability.

I. SPEAK UP ABOUT SPECIAL QUALITIES

Conference speaker Cindy Tobias says she makes a point of saying to her son, "You know what I like about you?" Then she proceeds to tell him.

How would you complete that thought if you were talking to your child? What can you compliment about his character—his work ethic, consideration for others, discipline, courage, originality, sense of humor? Whatever quality you recognize, encourage your child by affirming that trait or behavior appropriately and often. In fact, make it a habit to often say to your child, "Do you know what I like about you?"

God gives individuals different talents in different quantities, "each according to his own ability" (Matthew 25:15). Not everyone has the same strengths, but everyone has *something*. As you look for things in your child that you can affirm, don't evaluate your child by the world's standard of success. Look for the intangible, internal qualities that God values above all else. Use them as foundation stones for building a strong and positive sense of worthiness in your child.

When Donald walked through the locker room, everyone stared. He loved it. All he wore was a pair of shorts and socks, strutting his perfectly chiseled body. To everyone's amusement, he stopped, kissed his own biceps, and crowed, "I love myself! I love myself!" Because everyone knew what a jokester he is, no one was offended by his antics. Everyone just laughed along with him. We knew he was obsessed with his physique, and just figured, well, that's Donald.

He definitely had worthability. It was easy for Donald to identify what made him special, because it was an external gift, obvious to the human eye. Most people's gifts, however, come from internal strengths. Harder to identify, they are treasures worth looking for. Some things to notice:

   making an effort to protect an important relationship

   valuing the feelings of others

   caring about personal appearance

   taking good care of a possession they value

   doing a good job at something—school, household chores, sports, hobbies

   being different—figuring out how to be themselves

   evidence of Christ in their lives

   evidence of the fruit of the Spirit (Galatians 5:22–23)

Watch your kid for a month, and note these things or anything else that represents a God-given attribute—even if it's a tiny seed waiting to be watered. When you catch your child being good, praise him for it.

2. VALUE YOUR CHILD'S INPUT

Robert and Maggie live in an upscale neighborhood. Like most parents, they have high standards for their children. They didn't assume that the relative safety of their area meant their kids could run free. So when their two daughters entered the teenage years, they decided to set up an accountability system for their social lives.

They began with simple rules outlining when to be home and when to check in by phone. When the girls proved faithful in those small requirements, they were given more freedom.

When new situations arose, the girls and their parents sat down together and discussed guidelines. The girls were invited to join in the decision-making process. Robert and Maggie shared their own concerns and fears honestly—and listened hard to their daughters' opposition to these fears.

Ultimately, Dad and Mom made the final judgment. But by including the girls in the process and taking their opinions seriously, they were able to agree on most guidelines. The girls knew they were respected by their parents and valued for their ideas and opinions. Their parents have also role modeled good decision-making skills based on biblical moral guidelines.

3. HIGHLIGHT YOUR CHILD'S HERITAGE

One of the worst phone calls I ever received was to tell me my grandfather had been diagnosed with cancer. Grandpa was a rock. He was my hero.

My grandfather's illness sent me back to old photos of his childhood. I began to see myself, where I came from, and where I could be going. I saw part of what made me who I am.

I admired my grandfather a great deal, but looking at his pictures gave me new pride in my family name. It made me want to live up to that name and maintain its integrity. For the first time, I understood the long road my grandfather had traveled, seeing his hard work and his faithfulness as a husband and father, and his smile captured on film as he stood outside the nightclub he owned and managed. His creativity and entrepreneurial spirit were known throughout his native Jamaica. Getting to know my grandfather helped me affirm gifts in myself.

Family heritage—knowing what came before us—can encourage, enlighten, and inspire. It can tell us who we are.

Take time to show your child old family albums and other records of family history. Your child may discover ancestors who had a passion to serve the Lord. He might learn about other talents or gifts he hasn't recognized in himself and become motivated to follow in someone's footsteps or fulfill unrealized dreams.

Or your child might find other kinds of answers by connecting with her roots. A young woman broke off an engagement because she didn't feel ready for marriage and wasn't sure about the young man. Much of her family was shocked and disappointed at her action, making her decision even more difficult. One day her grandmother sat her down and told her a similar story. "I was your age, honey," she said gently, "when I did the same thing. Everyone took it hard, and no one understood me either. But I knew I had done the right thing because a year or so later I met your grandfather. That time I knew it was right."

What encouragement that young woman gained from learning a little tidbit of family history!

4. TELL THE TRUTH ABOUT FAMILY TROUBLES

While you help your child learn about her family, don't be afraid to tell the truth—even unpleasant family secrets—when you feel your children are mature enough to understand. Obviously, there are ways you can share this information with respect. There's no need to disparage old Uncle Fred or Aunt Edna. Tell only what will benefit the faith and growth of your child.

The Bible says the sins of the fathers are passed down to future generations. A history of abuse, alcoholism, drug use, or other vices can influence a family for generations. When children are affected by these things but don't know why, they struggle with issues that have no answers. If being able to communicate honestly and lovingly has not been the norm for your family tree, for example, it probably won't be the norm for your child. Yet if your child understands how her family's past contributes to the hard time she has with relationships or trusting others, she might be able to break the cycle.

THE POWER of BELIEVING in YOUR CHILD

The truth will set you free, Jesus said. Knowing family secrets helps kids grapple with the truth that people struggle, make mistakes, and suffer bad things—yet people survive. Children can learn how God was faithful through the generations to protect their ancestors. They see how people paid for their trespasses in heartbreaking ways.

Remember, what you try to hide from your child will eventually be found out. Your child would rather hear ugly family facts from you than from a chain of gossip. Trusting him with private information affirms his maturity, and learning that family members can love each other through good and bad times reinforces his security.

SHOW THE WAY

THE BEST EXAMPLE

Jesus was about to face one of His life's biggest battles. Forty days and nights in the wilderness—fasting and praying—led up to the launch of His earthly ministry. The devil was waiting because the stage was set for Jesus to begin the most significant three years of His earthly life.

As a sign of His readiness, Jesus came from Galilee to the Jordan River to be baptized by John the Baptist. Even though John tried to refuse Him—John figured he should be baptized by Jesus—Jesus responded, "Let it be so," and John complied.

At that moment, the heavens opened up, the Spirit of God descended like a dove, and the voice of God announced to the world, "This is My beloved Son, whom I love, and with whom I am well pleased."

Why do you think Jesus, the Son of God, needed to be affirmed or encouraged? He was sure of His identity. He had no doubts about His life's goals. But this is an example we can't afford to miss. God encouraged His Son in front of the whole world. He let everyone know He was standing by His Son. If the Son of God received affirmation from His Father as He launched into His life's work, surely our kids deserve to have their worthability reinforced with the same kind of encouragement.

CHAPTER SIX

DESTINED TO...
HAVE COURAGE

> *Courage is not simply one of the virtues but the form of every virtue at the testing point, which means at the point of highest reality.*

C. S. LEWIS

Short, slightly built—with an attitude. That was Z, the European kid whose family had recently moved to America. Adjusting to his new home and school of three thousand students was complicated by the pack of bullies who harassed him regularly. Z didn't feel much like he fit into his new environment—or into life for that matter.

When I met him, I learned that he was a typical no-friends outcast. But I was having my own attitude that day.

I had just finished preaching at a large church. The whole time I spoke, a group of kids huddled in a corner talking and laughing. When I invited kids to step up to make a stand for Christ or ask for prayer, only five came forward—out of two hundred kids. The angels are kind enough to rejoice when one person comes to the Lord, but I was irritated. "I have a roomful of pagans who need God," I grumbled. They should have repented for being rude!

My bad attitude almost caused me to dismiss Z and neglect his real needs. As bad as his situation was on that day he became a Christian, it got worse.

At first, accepting Christ didn't change Z's life. He was sincere but not serious. He still got picked on at school. He felt even more miserable when he started getting stomachaches. The recurring pain finally forced him to see a doctor. What his family assumed was just a nervous stomach turned out to be a rare, virulent cancer. He flew to a hospital three thousand miles away for six weeks of intensive treatment. He returned weakened and discouraged, his future uncertain. He was ready to give up.

In his despair, Z remembered the night he asked Jesus into his life. He reached out to God and slowly began to build a relationship with the Lord through Bible study and prayer. He began to experience answers to his prayers and developed a dogged passion to enter school sports. His courage in pursuing athletics in spite of his health problems earned him the respect of his peers. He was voted Athlete of the Year. And as the cancer tried to defeat his body, Z continued to grow stronger spiritually. He seldom let his health problems hinder him. He volunteered at our crusade where I preached, working tirelessly even in the midst of extreme nausea and fatigue from chemo treatments.

His doctors finally told him they wanted to try to remove the tumor, but couldn't say whether removal would work or even help. When they opened up Z, the tumor practically fell out. The doctors called the lack of attachments to surrounding tissue unexplainable, given the nature of the cancer. Z called it a miracle.

BE OF GOOD CHEER

GOOD COURAGE

Z is now a student at Brown University, and his drive for serving God influences other young men and women. When I think about how badly he suffered for so long, I realize that God made him brave to face the ultimate test and, as C. S. Lewis said, the highest reality.

Z rose above his circumstances because he had the courage to live even in the face of dying.

What enables some people, like Z, to face difficult circumstances courageously, while others crumble under the same pressures? Cowardly Lion thought the Wizard of Oz could just hand courage to him like a new shirt. Put it on, and you're brave! But the lion learned there was more to it than that. So must our kids.

The word "courage" is rooted in the Greek word *tharsos*, which means "to be of good cheer, be confident, or bold." That confidence and boldness can apply to an action taken or truth to be believed. Courage is a broad synonym for brave, valiant, heroic, lionhearted, undaunted, undismayed, bold, daring, firm, gutsy, nervy—to list just a few related qualities.

Courage makes people keep going even in the face of failure or death. In this strange and sometimes hostile world, your children need courage. They may never fight to escape a housing project or survive big city streets, or battle drug addiction or life-threatening illness. But some will. And all children need courage to succeed and survive.

God has destined our children to be brave.

God commands courage. Back in the Old Testament, Joshua faced an awesome task: cross the Jordan River and conquer the Promised Land. There were troops to move, people to feed, deadly enemies to conquer, and a land to settle. Joshua had plenty of reasons to be afraid! Yet God commanded him to be courageous. "Have I not commanded you? Be strong and of good courage; do not be afraid, nor be dismayed, for the Lord your God is with you wherever you go" (Joshua 1:9). God's promise of courage is wrapped up in His commands. Joshua could charge ahead with confidence because he was doing what God had told him to do.

God bestows courage. We don't cook up courage on our own. Better than anyone, God knows our weakness and the strength He must build in us to face life boldly. The writer of Hebrews, speaking of Jesus, tells us, "We do not have a High Priest who cannot sympathize with our weaknesses, but was in all points tempted as we are, yet without sin" (Hebrews 4:15). God stood in our place and felt our fears. He allowed himself to become human and be tempted with the same trials that we experience.

God promises all the courage we will ever need. God promises in His Word that He will never give any of us more than we can handle: "God is faithful; he will not let you be tempted beyond what you can bear. But when you are tempted, he will also provide a way out so that you can stand up under it" (1 Corinthians 10:13, NIV). God will allow nothing to befall His children for which He hasn't already given them the courage to handle.

Knowing this truth, we can be confident that God wants to give our children boundless courage and strength to resist temptation and boldness to face any circumstance without fear. Young people with God-given courage will resist peer pressure to experiment with drugs, sex, gangs, or other harmful activities. Courage and boldness will be their allies when they apply for college or a job or try out for a school play or athletic team. Courage will carry them through heartbreaking experiences.

I passionately believe that our children are destined to greatness, and there can be no greatness without courage. Winston Churchill said, "Courage . . . is the quality which guarantees all others."

WRONG ROAD

BAD COURAGE

If God has "good courage" to give us or teach us, is there "bad courage"? I think so.

Misguided courage pushes kids into doing harmful things. Peer pressure and society's skewed standards enable young people to apply courage to wrongdoing. Emulating the antiheroes in movies, television, and music can make a kid feel brave and daring and bold.

According to the Children's Defense Fund, every day in the United States the following is true:

- Misguided courage causes 500 adolescents to start using drugs and another 1,000 kids to begin drinking alcohol.

- Ignorant courage pushes 2,200 teenagers to drop out of high school.
- Foolish courage causes 135,000 kids to bring weapons or guns to school. Many of these kids join gangs, thinking there is some kind of future to hanging out on street corners selling drugs.
- False courage convinces 1,106 teenage girls to get abortions and 6 teenagers to commit suicide.

These statistics aren't compiled from troubled kids. They reflect the experience of the general teenage population, including kids from two-parent, churchgoing homes.

GIVING UP

NO COURAGE

If there's good courage and bad courage, there's also the absence of courage. While some kids look for good and bad opportunities to demonstrate guts, other young people run from confrontation. They have been robbed of opportunities to be courageous. So when things get tough, they can't make it.

Johnny was a teammate my freshman year of college. He was completely set up with a brand new car, $1,500 stereo, and gym equipment in his apartment—just in case he didn't feel like working out with other people. Whatever Johnny wanted, he called home and it was paid for. He had worked for none of his wealth, so he had no idea how to take care of things for himself.

His ignorance and lack of drive showed up during football practice. He tended to flee when things got tough—like the pursuit drill, which required eleven players to run forty yards over and over in pursuit of an imaginary ball carrier. We ran the full drill five times in about ten minutes, so it was exhausting. Johnny was in my group, and one day I knew he wasn't going make it. With each turn he lagged farther behind, and when he finally reached the huddle, he collapsed in tears, complaining about being tired. The next day he quit the team.

Quitting at football is one thing. Giving up on life is another. Young people need our help to learn how not to quit when things get tough. Things inevitably get tough—that's a promise! "In the world you will have tribulation," Jesus said, "but be of good cheer, I have overcome the world" (John 16:33). When our kids know they have Jesus by their side and when they know He will allow nothing they can't endure, then they can run and run and keep on running when there is nothing left to run with. If they have never stuck it out through life's pursuit drills, they won't know what it means to suck it up and fight through. They won't be equipped to be courageous— to stand up for their faith, to endure ridicule and do right, to work through relationship problems, or to pursue dreams despite failure and discouragement.

FUELED BY FAITH

GIANT KILLER

King David wasn't always a king. He never even got to practice as a prince. He was a shepherd boy, destined by God for great things.

When David was still an adolescent, the prophet Samuel visited his home. Jesse, David's father, introduced the old prophet to all his older, "successful" sons. Samuel was searching for the future king of Israel, but to not one of these handsome specimens of manhood did God say, "Yes, this is my man."

Perplexed, Samuel turned to Jesse and asked, "Are all the young men here?"

Jesse replied, "There remains yet the youngest; there he is, keeping the sheep."

"Bring him," Samuel responded.

As soon as Samuel saw David, the Lord said to him, "Anoint him, for this is the one!"

Samuel prayed for David, anointed him with oil, and, as the Bible says, "the Spirit of the Lord came upon David."

Many years passed before David actually took the throne, but the Lord began to prepare him for leadership. The day God poured His

Spirit upon him, David's destiny began to be fulfilled.

Shortly afterward, David became aware of Goliath's threats to his people. No one yet took Samuel's anointing seriously. David was still the youngest, still just a shepherd boy. His father sent him with bread and cheese to the battlefront—to his soldier brothers, but when he overheard the men discussing the situation, he grew impatient with their lack of action. "Who is this uncircumcised Philistine that he should defy the armies of the living God?" he cried indignantly. He was ready to fight.

His brothers told him to get lost. "Why did you come down here?" Eliab, the oldest, said irritably. They considered his shepherding a boy's job. They, after all, were soldiers, doing a man's job.

When David went to King Saul and declared that he would fight Goliath, Saul also gave him a hard time. "You can't go against this Philistine," he said, "You are but a youth and he a man of war. . . ."

No one believed in David, but David believed in God. His courage was fueled by faith. He defeated the giant and became a national hero.

What David's brothers and others couldn't have known was that during those long hours tending sheep God had prepared David for his destiny. When David wrote, "The Lord is my shepherd," in Psalm 23, he was writing from personal experience. David wasn't just shuffling sheep. He was learning to shepherd God's people.

The small responsibilities in our children's lives are God's plan for preparing them for their futures. Household chores, discipline in schoolwork, jobs, sports, tending sheep—whatever—teaches them to be faithful and to follow through. That faithfulness will translate into confidence, boldness, and courage.

EYES OF FAITH

NO FEAR!

If you had been David's mom or dad and you had followed him out to the battlefield, worrying like parents do, what would you have seen? Probably the same thing all the soldiers saw: a 9' 9" giant—

awesome size and strength intimidating to even the bravest warriors.

What do you think David saw? He saw the same big bully, but his eyes and heart were focused on the awesome might and power of God.

David didn't care how big Goliath was. Read how he taunted him: "This day the Lord will deliver you into my hand. I will strike you and take your head from you. . . . I will give the carcasses of the camp of the Philistines to the birds of the air and the wild beasts of the earth, that all the earth may know that there is a God in Israel" (1 Samuel 17:46).

That kid had no fear!

Young people attempt things that scare adults because the young haven't lost their childlike faith. As adults, we see giants in the land. We want to protect our children but we also need to be careful not to poison their faith with our fears. Every generation has new battles to fight. It's important, then, to look back at our own cowardice and courage and understand where our fears come from. Before you call your child back from the battles of life, ask yourself these questions:

Where in life have I been courageous? Have I shared those successes with my child?

- When did I give up? Have I modeled fear for my child?
- Were there instances in which it was good that I ran away or quit?
- How do I tell my child it's okay to try hard and fail?
- Am I expecting my child to make up for opportunities I missed because I lacked courage?
- When did I show bad courage? If my child knows about this, how have I communicated the cost of misplaced courage?
- How are my fears different from my child's fears?
- What boundaries have I set around my child to keep him safe?
- Do I automatically guard against new things?
- What have I accomplished in life that my parents didn't?
- In what areas does my child need to outdo me—and am I holding him back?

MOVING FORWARD

COLORS OF COURAGE

These questions hint at some crucial facts about courage: No child will be courageous in every aspect of life. No child will show the exact same type of courage as his parents showed. And courage always varies according to the gifts God has given us.

Courage is the quality that causes us to venture forth, to move forward, to do new things. Different times and places call for different doses of courage. God will show His strength through each generation according to its needs, and through each child according to His plan. Let's look at the varieties of courage God might grant your child.

LIFE-GIVING COURAGE

Mario's role models during his growing-up years epitomized evil. His father and mother were heroin addicts who introduced him to drugs when he was only eight years old. His uncles and other relatives were thieves, drug dealers, and gang members. Prison was a revolving door Mario passed through on at least eight occasions. He dabbled in satanism, which drew him deeper into darkness, violence, and drugs. To his peers, Mario was a courageous, dangerous man, a tough guy who shot people for crossing him. No one thought he was afraid of anything or anybody.

The true test of Mario's courage began the day he found his father dying from a heroin/cocaine overdose. Reality crashed down on him as he discovered that one of his relatives had tried to kill his dad with the lethal combination.

By now Mario's mother had turned her life around, and as she saw her son struggling and searching for truth, she invited him to church. That day he heard the Gospel and decided to follow Christ— and began a crusade for the truth.

Inspired by a new kind of courage, Mario confronted the murderous relative who had tried to kill his dad. When the relative threatened Mario's life, Mario challenged his family to examine their lives and listen to the Gospel. He visited the hospital to share his new faith with his dad. Continued opposition from his former gang and his family puts Mario's life in constant danger, but for him, going backward isn't an option. He knows firsthand the consequences of disobeying God, and he now considers following God his only choice.

His genuine change of heart has given him a burden for what is the most difficult ministry he could take on: his own vengeful and violent family. Most of them would sooner see him dead than serving the Lord. Mario was a tough guy before, but now he is displaying courage that builds up instead of tearing down.

DAILY COURAGE

Watch for instances in your child's everyday life when courage shows. It may not be as obvious or dramatic as it is in Mario's situation, but there might be more to be proud of than you realize.

I remember when the six-year-old daughter of some friends decided she was ready to be baptized. The church her family attended held their baptisms in the Pacific Ocean, usually on a sunny California day with lots of fellowship and family picnicking. But this day the weather and water turned cold, and the usually calm bay was churned up by stormy waves.

The mom looked at her skinny, shivering little girl, knowing she was afraid of big waves, and told her she could wait for a better day. "But today I am ready to follow Jesus," her daughter responded, and she marched out into the water where her pastor stood waiting to baptize her. She came up teeth chattering but smiling. In her own little world, she had done a very brave thing.

Each time your child confronts a difficult, uncomfortable, or fearful situation, she is exercising courage. Watch for these things:
    confronting wrong or unrighteous behavior
    acting out of the norm for their peers for the sake of doing right
    taking on new challenges you know will be difficult or fearful
    persistence in completing a task or project, even when everyone
        else tells them to give up (remember Noah)

122

doing the right thing, like sticking up for the kid who gets picked
   on

ignoring ridicule

walking away from unhealthy relationships

Remember Cowardly Lion? It wasn't until Wizard of Oz pointed out to him all the brave things he had done during his journey on the yellow brick road that he finally realized he had courage.

PERSISTENT COURAGE

Courage says no to defeat—sometimes over and over again. One big, dramatic, brave act of courage might be easier to accomplish than persistence in the face of defeat.

Katie was a typical seventh grader with a sincere desire to play volleyball. Out for the junior high team, she soon discovered that whatever it took to play volleyball she didn't have. She couldn't jump, couldn't hit the ball when she swung at it, couldn't serve—and she had no experience whatsoever.

But Katie was determined. The next year was no better. She got rotated out more often than in, and most of her teammates sighed when she walked onto the court.

The following summer she spent every weekend practicing with her dad in the park. She came back to school an improved player but was held back on the JV team, while all her friends got bumped up to varsity.

Katie kept at it. She made the varsity team and became a respectably good player. What was most impressive about her game was her keep-coming-back-for-more determination. Persistent courage gets up again and again without worrying about what others think or what happens in the end. Volleyball won't make or break Katie's life, but her ability to display courage in the midst of failure will surely be played out in an even more significant arena later in her life.

FAITHFUL COURAGE

Holding on to the promises of God is perhaps the greatest form of courage. As Karle Baker has said, "Courage is fear that has said its prayers."

I met Justine when she attended my youth group in high school. She was a normal, healthy teenager—refreshing to see—who went to football games, school dances, and hung out at the beach. She attended church faithfully and was just nice to have around. I was excited for her when she came back later to tell me she was engaged. Christmas 1996 was supposed to be the best of her life.

Two days before Christmas, her right hand and foot started feeling numb. A trip to the doctor and a CAT scan resulted in immediate surgery to remove a cancerous tumor from the left side of her brain. Swiftly her "normal" world was transformed as she began a regimen of chemotherapy and hospitalizations. For the first time in her young life, death became a reality. Prayer became her main pastime as she struggled to find peace and hope.

I watched Justine transformed through her suffering into a woman of faith and courage. She held on to and believed with all her being the words of 2 Corinthians 5:6–8: "We are always confident, knowing that while we are at home in the body we are absent from the Lord. For we walk by faith, not by sight. We are confident, yes, well pleased rather to be absent from the body and to be present with the Lord."

Courage isn't always measured by how boldly we conquer obstacles but rather by how firmly and confidently we hang on to the promises of God. Justine learned that life doesn't always go the way we expect it to. She was honest about her fears and pain, believing that the ultimate failure in the eyes of the world—death—would one day be the ultimate victory for her as a believer. She declared along with the apostle Paul, "For to me, to live is Christ, and to die is gain" (Philippians 1:21).

ENOUGH IS ENOUGH
BALANCING COURAGE WITH WISDOM

Ben started boxing when he was still a teenager. As a resident of the Bronx in New York City, Ben's ultimate goal was to box in the Golden Gloves Tournament. A slender Puerto Rican guy with a ten-inch Afro and fearfully pale skin, he didn't fit the boxer image. But he tried. He made it to the Golden Gloves but, unfortunately, Ben wasn't too good.

During the 1986 New York City Golden Gloves Tournament, Ben was knocked down. Often when the referee comes over to give the standing eight count, he tells the fighter he's going to stop the fight, as a precautionary measure. He does this to test the fighter's heart and his willingness to go on. Ninety-nine times out of a hundred, the boxer says, "No, I'm OK," and gets up. But as Ben lay on the floor, he weighed his options. He could get up and have a remote chance of toughing it out and winning the fight, or he could get hurt really bad.

Ben the boxer said, "Yeah, I think stopping is a good idea."

It may look like Ben was a quitter. But in reality he was wise.

Courage can't always fight on. Courage also knows when enough is enough—even when it means a humiliating walk to the locker room. In the ring, Ben discovered he wasn't meant to be a boxer— and he had no good reason to risk permanent injury. His courage wasn't in question. His wisdom was. Ben went on to display an enormous amount of courage in his life as a New York City police officer.

Sometimes when a kid gets knocked down, he won't get up. It's your job to be sensitive to his reasons and redirect his life toward something more compatible with his gifts and calling. Kids don't always have the sense, though, to stop. For Ben it was easy. He got tired of getting beat up.

MAKE WAY
ENCOURAGING COURAGE

Courage is an intangible quality. We usually recognize it when we see it but we don't always know how to go about developing it.

I want to leave you with a few ideas, saying again at the start that it's crucial to pray and ask God how to recognize and encourage courage in your children.

I. LET YOUR CHILD EXPERIENCE ADVERSITY

Seanne's parents could give her anything. An excellent student with strong motivation to become a lawyer, Seanne applied and was accepted to the college of her choice. To her surprise, her parents sat her down and told her she would have to find a way to pay for her education on her own.

They realized Seanne would struggle. Her desire to practice law would be tested severely. But they also felt that this experience was the best way for her to develop the courage to follow her dream effectively.

Some may think this was extreme. But in a situation where a child has never truly struggled, this structured, deliberate adversity might be a wise decision. Her parents prayed for her and encouraged her, and she learned to depend upon God for her resources, not Mom and Dad. Seanne is now an attorney licensed in two states.

Some lessons are only learned through hard times. "We also glory in tribulations," the apostle Paul wrote, "knowing that tribulation produces perseverance; and perseverance, character; and character, hope. Now hope does not disappoint, because the love of God has been poured out in our hearts by the Holy Spirit who was given to us" (Romans 5:3–5). God, the loving Father, carefully allows us to go through hard times so we will grow and be strengthened by them. Seanne's loving earthly father knew how to allow courage to develop in his daughter.

2. GIVE YOUR CHILD INDEPENDENCE

As great as premarital counseling can be, nothing teaches a husband and wife to get along like experiencing marriage firsthand. Likewise, your child won't grow confident without experiencing the other normal changes and challenges of life firsthand. You can provide your child with a head start while he's still under your watchful eye if, as part of your child's training for leaving home, you give him opportunities to do things by himself. Some ideas:

go on a job interview

hold down a job

confront problem situations with adults and peers

travel to another town, state, or country

start his own business

raise money for a good cause

take care of someone else (e.g., child or elderly person)

share the Gospel in public

For more ideas, start a journal of specific things that scared or surprised you as you got out on your own. Make it your goal to help your child begin to master those things as he grows toward maturity.

3. ENCOURAGE BOLD FAITH

Children and teenagers have a lot to say and do in the cause of courageously advancing God's kingdom. Even though they also have a lot to learn, they have unlimited potential. Look at your child and ask yourself:

How does my child see life? As something to be feared or a challenge to be met?

How much courage does she have to take on the giants in her life?

How would she confront bullies?

How does my child view church and the problems there?

How could she share her faith with her friends?

How could she make church more fun, exciting, and appealing to her peers?

Have I challenged her to pray for our church?

Do I give her the opportunity to do "adult" ministry?

Is she willing to speak out on her campus? Teach a Bible study? Start a Bible club?

What do these things have to do with courage? Everything. It takes guts for a kid to step out of his or her youth-oriented world and step up into more adult responsibilities. Most kids enjoy the challenge, and, given the opportunity, most go for it. Look again at some of the biblical examples of youthful courage and discuss them with your kids:

Timothy was a young man when Paul sent him to resolve several serious issues in the church at Ephesus. Perhaps Paul himself could have rushed back to Ephesus to set everyone straight. They would, after all, quickly listen to him. But instead, he commissioned Timothy to go, advising him, "Let no one despise your youth, but be an example to the believers in word, in conduct, in love, in spirit, in faith, in purity" (1 Timothy 4:12). In other words, do boldly what you are called to do, Tim, and don't let anyone tell you you're too young.

When Solomon was pronounced king, he cried out to the Lord, "I am a little child . . ." (1 Kings 3:7). He was afraid. He knew he couldn't do the job alone, so he called on God and rose to the occasion.

Jeremiah was called to be a prophet and protested fearfully. "I cannot speak," he told God, "for I am a youth." God would have none of that. "Do not be afraid . . ." He responded, "for I am with you to deliver you" (Jeremiah 1:6, 8).

That last Scripture is the key to courage. "For I am with you," God promised. Jesus promises us today, "I am with you always."

When your child knows without a doubt that God is with her, then no matter how big the giant, she won't be afraid. Take time right now to pray for your child. Each child has been called by God to do something uniquely designed for him or her. God is looking for people with passion for His work, and that passion may lie in the heart of your child. Look at your child with faith, believing that God has destined her for something great and special and that He will give her the courage to follow Him.

4. ALLOW ROOM TO FAIL

Many people I know are exceptional parents, working hard to provide good, safe, loving homes for their children. Sometimes things are too good. If courage is the ability to move past fear and failure, kids will never learn it unless they are allowed the opportunity to step out, to fail, or to lose.

I play UNO with my kids a lot. It's a simple card game we can all play—and I play to win! Even though my kids were young when we started, I told them they would have to work to win. There'd be no going easy for them. I was playing to win and it was going to get ugly.

They acted all nervous and called their mom, but I'd answer, "She can't help you. You're all mine. You want to win? Then you have to work for it."

Before long they started telling me they were going to beat me. Pretty soon they *were* beating me. All the time. They learned to overcome being intimidated by Dad—I don't think they were ever too afraid of me—and they learned to win with their own strategies and defenses.

Winning a game of UNO may seem insignificant, but it became a simple exercise for my kids to learn that things aren't always going to be easy. Life gets ugly and hard, and as parents, we need to resist the temptation to make hard things go away. Courage only develops in adversity.

WHAT'S IT FOR?

YOU ONLY NEED COURAGE IN THE FACE OF FEAR

In what context do you witness courage being manifested? Easy times? Good times? Kickback times? Obviously not. Courage rises to the surface in times of adversity.

A friend of mine says that growing up he was quiet and sensitive. He hated competition. He despised physical risk. He can't think of anything he did in childhood that truly pushed him to be courageous. It took him until late junior high to discover the sport of soccer, where his teammates labeled him "all aggress and no finesse." In high school, he developed the courage to stand in front of a group and speak, which he did on a two-month mission trip with a bunch of teens and adults he had never met. In college, he gained independence by studying overseas. He became a pastor and learned how to lead. As an adult, he's discovered he is actually highly competitive. He will kindly but brutally "do in" his adversaries on the racquetball court. He's an avid cyclist, and he hates to get beat. Once, on a recreational ride, he fell in line behind a group of five guys on titanium road bikes. He kept the pace for miles on a mountain bike—*with* his two-year-old son on the bike's carrier.

My friend claims that the meanest thing his parents ever did was be nice to him. What he means is that he had no nasty homelife to toughen him up for the real world. As an adult, he is still sensitive but he has acquired a courageous edge that lets him face challenges, speak his mind, share his faith, and go eyeball-to-eyeball with peers. Raising his own kids, he looks for ways to challenge them to try difficult, unusual things.

As our kids launch out on their own, we can't always be there to hold their hands. Even the quietest life is full of hard things. Our hands need to open to release them and fold to pray for them, asking God to give them the courage to stand against the winds of opposition wherever they may go.

"Be strong in the Lord and in the power of His might. Put on the whole armor of God, that you may be able to stand" (Ephesians 6:10–11).

DESTINED TO. . . .
STAND

> **"**
>
> *It is impossible to comprehend the adolescent mind
> without understanding this terror of the peer group.*
> **"**

DR. JAMES DOBSON

Historians researching Nazi Germany discovered a chilling phenomenon. Many of the German soldiers responsible for executing hundreds, even thousands of Jews were not brutal SS troops. They were average, politically indifferent citizens, mostly shopkeepers and factory workers who had been drafted into the army.

As the war neared the end, some of the SS commanders grew weary of the slaughter and gave the soldiers the option to change duties. The majority of these men chose to continue the executions, the researchers discovered, out of fear of being ridiculed by their peers!

If the powerful force of peer pressure can cause grown men to perform brutal acts of evil, imagine what our kids are up against (Gary Bauer, *Our Journey Home*, Word, 162).

DARE TO STAND

SITTING APART FROM THE CROWD

Twelve-year-old Kendall, looking forward to her first real soccer game after weeks of practice, arrived at the field to find something strange going on.

The coach had asked the girls to sit in a circle in the middle of the field and meditate. With their fingers connected, they began to hum and chant over and over, "We will win the soccer game, we will win the soccer game. . . ."

Kendall instinctively reacted with discomfort. What her coach had asked certainly didn't seem compatible with her Christian up-bringing. She struggled with what to do, not wanting to make a scene. She chose to quietly sit on the outside of the circle and pray. Her teammates weren't happy. They called her names and tried to taunt her into joining them. Kendall didn't want to disappoint her friends, but she wanted to stay faithful to God.

When Kendall's mother discovered what was going on, she confronted the coach, whose wife promised that it wouldn't happen again. But it did happen again—at every single game for several weeks. Each week Kendall's resolve was tested as she sat outside the circle. Her parents prayed and let her know they supported her. They realized that she needed to be allowed to go through this because courage, character, and the ability to withstand peer pressure were being developed in her life.

All young people face peer pressure, and *all* of them are capable of resisting it—but only if they have the encouragement and prayers of people who understand this potent force in kids' lives.

WHO TO IMPRESS?

THE TERROR OF PEERS

A peer is someone considered an equal or like-minded companion. For many young people, the relationship is more hopeful than real. They *wish* they were on equal social, athletic, or academic standing with that other person. The real pressure comes when there is tension, obligation, or urgency to make that friend-to-friend fit happen. Young people have a deep need to feel equal and accepted; consequently, they feel *a deep fear of disappointing others.*

One of the most essential bits of information you can gather about your child is whom he wants to impress—or, looked at another way, whom he fears disappointing. That fear of displeasing or being rejected by others is the key to peer pressure, and knowing the source of your child's pressure will give you information to help him stand against it. Later in this chapter, we'll discuss ways you can influence whom your kid wants to please.

From a parent's perspective, God, parents, and other good role models are worth pleasing. For many kids, however, greater behavioral pressure comes from their natural peers.

Natural peers are in our kids' lives because of age and convenience. As soon as children go to school or join a team, club, youth group, or other activity they are confronted with peers they look up to or don't want to disappoint. They want to be accepted and liked.

Kids' actions are strongly influenced by their need to be accepted by the social power brokers in their world, the kids who are masters at exploiting the peer pressure phenomenon: the popular ones, the "in" crowd, the big "they." I remember how they made me feel my social standing was forever doomed if I did anything to disappoint them. It took a lot of maturing to realize the people I feared were masters of illusion. Behind their social masks, the social elite are just as insecure and needy as everyone else. But other kids don't know that and can suffer for years feeling rejected by the "important" people.

Dr. James Dobson explains peer fear this way:

> There are two great forces that combine to create havoc during adolescence, the first having a hormonal origin. The other is social in nature. It is common knowledge that a twelve- or thirteen-year-old child suddenly awakens to a brand new world around him, as though his eyes were opening

for the first time. The world is populated by age mates who scare him out of his wits. His greatest anxiety, far exceeding the fear of death, is the possibility of rejection or humiliation in the eyes of his peers. . . . It is impossible to comprehend the adolescent mind without understanding this terror of the peer group.

What society and our kids' peers establish as cool obviously is often vastly different from what we as parents think is important. Unless someone establishes higher credibility and a better standard, kids will bow to false gods.

SUPREME TEST
THE FIERY FURNACE

Imagine this scenario for a moment: you're a teenager, and a foreign army invades your home, destroys your city, slaughters your family, and kidnaps you and three of your friends. Instead of being brutally murdered like the rest, your little group is taken into the king's household, offered fine clothes, food, and accommodations, plus an all-expenses-paid graduate education and a guaranteed position in the king's court. The price for this privileged life? A complete renunciation of your former life. You swap your God for your captors' gods and forsake your family, heritage, faith, and culture. If you refuse—well, they have no use for you. You and your friends will be thrown into an oven and burned alive.

Some choice! What would you do? What would your teenagers do?

That wild scenario is what actually played out in 605 B.C. when the Babylonian armies of King Nebuchadnezzar besieged Jerusalem, destroying everything in sight—except, as the king ordered, "young men in whom there was no blemish, but good-looking, gifted in all wisdom, possessing knowledge and quick to understand . . ." (Daniel 1:4). Daniel, Hananiah, Mishael, and Azariah matched that description, and soon found themselves swept into Babylonian life.

Their names were changed to Belteshazzar, Shadrach, Meshach, and Abed-Nego. They were taught the language and literature of the Chaldeans and eventually promoted to the king's inner circle of advisors.

In spite of their advancement, these four young men clung to a remnant of their former lives. They kept their faith and refused to bow to the pressures of the world system. Nebuchadnezzar stole them physically from their homes and heritage, but he could not steal their hearts. He couldn't alter their relationship with God.

They were put to the test in many ways—you've heard of Daniel in the lion's den?—but on one particular occasion, Shadrach, Meshach, and Abed-Nego were specifically singled out for refusing to worship Nebuchadnezzar's golden idols (Daniel 3:1–30). The king was so furious he not only sentenced them to the fiery furnace but ordered the fire to be stoked up to seven times its usual intensity.

GOOD EXAMPLE

GANG FOR GOOD

Shadrach, Meshach, and Abed-Nego were a good example of the right kind of peer pressure. They made a commitment and were faithful to it, even in the face of death. How could such young men have such resolve? They had faith in God, and they had each other.

Given their drastic situation, they could easily have told themselves it was okay to give up and commit suicide, like too many kids do today—as evidenced by the 300 percent increase in the number of teenage suicides in our country since the 1950s. They had good reason to run away—like 1.5 million kids in this country do every year. They could have turned into a gang for evil, fought in the streets to vent their fear and frustration, and wound up dead like the gang kids of today—and enough are being killed today to make homicide a leading cause of teen deaths in the U.S.

But Shadrach, Meshach, and Abed-Nego chose not to crumble under the pressure. After the furnace was fired up, King Nebuchadnezzar commanded his soldiers to toss in the three young men. Because the fire had been stoked to extraordinary temperatures, the soldiers themselves were killed by the blast of heat.

Taking one last look at his vanquished foes, Nebuchadnezzar peered into the furnace and was astonished. "Did we not cast three men bound into the midst of the fire?" he asked his counselors.

"True, O king," they responded.

"Look!" he answered, "I see four men loose, walking in the midst of the fire; and they are not hurt, and the form of the fourth is like the Son of God" (Daniel 3:24–25).

The king was pretty perceptive. He knew who that fourth figure was. God himself was in the fire with Shadrach, Meshach, and Abed-Nego. Even a pagan king recognized the power of the true God. That day he promoted the three young men and declared that they should be harmed by no one ever, "because there is no other God who can deliver like this."

STICK TOGETHER

LOYAL FRIENDS

The Bible says friends keep friends sharp: "As iron sharpens iron, so a man sharpens the countenance of his friend" (Proverbs 27:17). The Bible also says friends don't let friends fall: "Two are better than one, because they have a good reward for their labor. For if they fall, one will lift up his companion. But woe to him who is alone when he falls, for he has no one to help him up. . . . Though one may be overpowered by another, two can withstand . . ." (Ecclesiastes 4:9–10, 12).

Those three Babylonian boys were loyal to each other. They were friends who stuck together and kept each other accountable to God and to their godly friendship. I'm sure that when Meshach missed his parents, Shadrach comforted him. When Shadrach was tempted by the king's food, Abed-Nego reminded him of their commitment to the Lord's diet. When Abed-Nego felt the first blast of heat from the fiery furnace, the others took his hand and shouted out their commitment to God. They held one another up during their hardest ordeals.

NO COMPROMISE

BABYLON STILL LIVES

You may be thinking, "I'm glad I don't live in a place where some king is trying to kill my family, kidnap and deport my kids, and wine and dine them into serving false gods." Think again. That is exactly what is happening in our culture today.

Satan is killing families through divorce, incest, and child abuse. He is kidnapping neighborhoods through gangs, drugs, and sexual immorality. He is trying to wine and dine our kids with the "good life"—parties, drugs, booze, ill-gotten wealth, sex with any willing partner. Children's minds are being filled with prideful thoughts of doing things their way—to use a biblical image, with thoughts of tasting of the tree of good and evil so they can know it all and be like little gods. Satan hasn't changed his tactics much since he beguiled Eve in the Garden of Eden. Over and over, kids get his old message, "You don't need to listen to your parents . . . the police . . . your teachers . . . and has God *really* said you can't do that?"

Is God really that uptight? Couldn't Shadrach, Meshach, and Abed-Nego have bowed just once to the king's idols—just to save their lives? Is one slip of disobedience that big a deal?

Our friends were wise young men. They knew that the system wouldn't be satisfied with a curtsey to the idols. Satan is never content. Evil is never full. One compromise leads to a lifetime of corruption. I'm sure those three agonized over their decision, but there never seemed any doubt what they would do. They wouldn't succumb to the pressure of their peers.

That no-compromise resolve is what we want to build into our kids.

Babylon is still alive and bent on brainwashing and ultimately destroying our kids. But that brainwashing is only possible to the degree that our children allow themselves to be deceived and bow to the false idols of this world. The final question is this: Will your child bow?

DON'T GIVE IN

NOT FOR SALE

When I was in high school, my friends and I played football in the park almost every weekend, rain or shine, mud or not. It was usually the same guys. We all knew who we did and did not want on our teams.

One guy always got picked last. "Tomp," we called him. He wasn't a bad player, just inconsistent. If he was having an off day, we left him uncovered when he went out for a pass. He wasn't much of a threat to score. There were guys, though, that we never left alone. Sometimes we covered them with two players because any time they got their hands on the ball they were sure to score.

Satan knows that youth have untapped potential. With a lifetime of service to God looming, they are a real threat to his dominion. When they're committed, they are in position to score a touchdown every time. That's why he hassles them so often. That's why he tries to get them thrown into life's fiery furnaces as often as possible. His tactic is to scare and discourage.

Even the kids we feel are way gone from God are a threat, because anything Satan can lure a kid into doing, God can redeem and one-up. If a fourteen-year-old girl can have a baby, she can also disciple baby Christians in a junior high fellowship. If Satan can entice a sixteen-year-old into shooting a gun and taking a life, God can use him to preach the Gospel that gives life. If an eighteen-year-old can be lured into the dangerous gang life of crime and violence, then Jesus can lead him through the valley of the shadow of death and teach him trust and compassion. If kids can find ways to get high and drunk and ruin their lives, then they can teach the Word of God that fills people with the joy of the Holy Spirit.

Shadrach, Meshach, and Abed-Nego knew they were already bought, owned, and not for sale. Before they were kidnapped, their commitment to God was well established. Satan daily tries to kidnap our kids and buy their affection. Yet once our kids have accepted the love of God and His ownership of their lives, they can send a message loud and clear: "We are not for sale!"

LOVE SHOWS

HUGS, KISSES, AND LOYALTIES

My son and youngest child is my wife's little baby. I can't believe how she pampers him! I'm trying to make him tough, and she undoes everything I do by treating him like a prince. She's constantly kissing him and telling him how much she loves him. He returns the affection eagerly.

One day she told me she was concerned about catching him in a lie. In fact, she questioned the truth of several statements he made to her that week. We did a little research and found he had indeed lied. While we were trying to figure out the correct discipline—she vetoed my suggestion of bread and water for a week—I decided that he needed to realize the hypocrisy of telling his mother he loves her, then turning around and lying to her.

His punishment for one week, therefore, was being prohibited from kissing his mother and telling her he loves her. We explained to him that lying and loving don't go together. He needed to learn that loving his mother means obeying her. We read him the Scripture about honoring his mother and father and told him that he hadn't done that when he lied.

He was crushed and repentant. His attitude showed us how important it is for him to be able to express love to his mother. He also learned more about the meaning of love and was deeply sorry he had disappointed us. And, yes, his dad is glad he knows how to give and receive affection.

Parents, deep inside every child is a desire to connect with Dad and Mom. Even kids who "hate" their parents long for their attention. (Youth workers call this "the soggy potato chip theory," that is, just as a soggy potato chip is better than no potato chip, a kid would rather have a bad parent than no parent.) One of the most important ways to help your children resist peer pressure is to teach them where their loyalties should lie—with you!

WORTHY TO PLEASE
STAY AT THE TOP OF THE LIST

If one of kids' greatest fears is disappointing others, they need to learn whom it's important not to disappoint. Help them distinguish who's earned their loyalty from who hasn't. Some people in their lives have earned the right to be at the top of the list, while others have bought it deceptively. Parents, you need to stay at the top of that "I want to please this person" list. Here are some ideas on how to do that:

1. Are you receptive to God's criticism and correction? I ask my kids once in a while to grade themselves. "How good have you been?" I ask them. Invariably, they respond, "I've been really good, Daddy."

"Okay, then, how do I know that? I can only gauge that by how well you are obeying me. Grade yourself based on how well you've completed the things I've asked you to do around the house."

When I put it like that, they usually walk away thinking real hard how to wiggle free. Likewise, let's ask ourselves how we would respond if our heavenly Father asked us to grade ourselves as parents. Have we been good?

God has given us a huge job around the house: nurturing a positive relationship with our children and modeling the love of Christ. If we get burned out from our adult life, letting ourselves get too tired, impatient, and hurried in our parenting, we fall down on following Ephesians 6:4: "Do not provoke your children to wrath, but bring them up in the training and admonition of the Lord."

Here's the simple truth: Children who come from positive, nurturing homes will struggle less with peer pressure, because they already know they are accepted by the people who mean the most to them.

2. Do you believe in the power of adults to influence your child? In spite of the tremendous influence of peer pressure in the adolescent years, *in the long run*, the number one influence in the life of a young person is almost always an adult. As a parent, you have more power than you will ever imagine. You also have the ability to invite other adults into your child's life.

Think about your childhood. List people who played the biggest roles in your life and had the most lasting influence. It's probably some adults who expressed special interest in you. Think about how badly you wanted to impress them and how much you hated to disappoint them.

There's an older lady at a local church whom several kids call their "church grandma." She makes a point of getting to know young people of all ages, from little ones to college age, and finds ways to show interest in their lives. Special gifts, contributions to their education or school projects, tea parties, notes and cards, picnics, long talks, and time to listen—she invests in these kids' lives. For a young lady with a passion for horses, she loaned money to buy a saddle, then taught her how to pay back a loan and handle finances. A college girl on her way to Europe was handed one hundred dollars and told, "Travel is the best education." This church grandma will turn up on a lot of lists of "adults who influenced my life."

Encourage your child's friendships with other adults you trust to influence your kids for good. Aunts and uncles, grandparents, friends, teachers, coaches, youth leaders—when your child respects someone other than his friends, he will desire to please them rather than succumb to peer pressure.

3. Are you constantly suspicious, critical, and negative? I bought a dental plan for my family that came with five free visits as part of the package. Once the free visits were used up, the benefits were gone and it was time to pay.

Maybe you've given your kids the benefit of the doubt, but their mistakes and sins have used up their benefits, your patience, and your grace, and now you want to make them pay.

Let them pay the consequences, but be careful you don't become a thumb-breaking bill collector.

What if I exceeded my dental plan's coverage because I took such poor care of my teeth? I'd expect my dentist to instruct me how to do better, chide me a little, then hand me the bill. I know I'm going to pay dearly for my neglect.

What if from now on, however, every time I bump into him at the grocery store or get my teeth cleaned, he yells, nags, and fires questions at me like, "What have you been eating?" "How often are you flossing?" "Why'd you wait so long to get in here?" "Just where do you think you're going with those teeth?" He'd lose me as a patient. And quick.

You get the idea. Don't criminalize every move your kid makes. Don't interrogate her the minute she walks into the house. Don't allow your relationship to be reduced to suspicion, doubt, and accusations. If she's used up her benefits, hand her the bill. Instruct her, then allow her to reap the consequences of her mistakes. But don't ever let her think she's losing you as a friend and cheerleader.

By the way, you should know that the benefits package works the other way as well. Parents have a benefits allowance with their kids. No parent is perfect, and with most kids you get a certain amount of harsh interrogations, critical accusations, and disappointing looks before you run out and your teenager starts looking for a different love-me-through-thick-and-thin supporter.

PARENTAL SUPPORT

STANDING WITH YOUR CHILD

Here are some suggestions, but each of the following ideas for motivating your child to please both God and the right kind of people is underwritten by one rule: Laugh. Dealing with peer fear and all the hurts and moral concerns it raises can be serious stuff. More than that, no one outgrows the need to feel like a carefree child once in a while. Get silly and pillow fight and have fun and tell jokes with your kid. Plan outings that are pure fun. Let your child see God's joy in your life and in his relationship with you. You aren't his peer, but you can always be his friend.

1. HELP YOUR KIDS REALIZE EVERYTHING ISN'T WHAT IT SEEMS

During the filming of a video on gangs, we interviewed about forty gang members. I was thoroughly surprised by what I heard.

The kids we interviewed readily admitted that their chances of getting arrested, not completing school, and getting killed before their twentieth birthday were greatly increased by gang membership. One kid acknowledged that joining means you're marked by other gangs as well as by the police, and you have to watch your back wherever you go.

"Then what good comes out of joining?" I asked.

"Nothing." Nothing good. Until they verbalized that thought, a lot of the kids we talked to hadn't stopped to think about what they were doing. Certainly, when I show that video to other kids it takes the glamour out of gang life.

When you meet kids that impress your child, take time to find out who they really are. Not only can the Lord use you to minister to those kids but you can also help your child view friends through a clearer, more objective lens. Peer pressure is like rose-colored glasses. What may look pretty can in reality be wretchedly ugly. Before your child decides to join in, he needs to see the truth.

2. PRAISE YOUR KIDS FOR MAKING RIGHT DECISIONS

When you witness your child resisting peer pressure, especially taking a stand for the right thing, reward her abundantly. Reinforce good behavior! After all, when we show courage in our attempts to obey God, He blesses us from a storehouse of immeasurable blessings. You can bless your child with a treat at the store, extra privileges at home, or a special time out with just Mom or Dad or both. Let her know you are pleased.

A potato chip company has a famous ad campaign that says, "Betcha can't eat just one." One of their commercials featured basketball players Kareem Abdul-Jabaar and Larry Bird. They had a bet. If either ate more than one, Larry had to shave his head, Kareem had to grow his hair—if he could. Larry ended up shaving his head. One chip led to a bagful.

Sin works the same way. In our human strength, it's a losing bet. Unfortunately, the temporary satisfaction of sin offers more than enough pleasure to get us to sin twice—and then again and again.

Shadrach, Meshach, and Abed-Nego learned as children that little concessions lead to bigger ones. If they bowed to one idol, they would bow to others and slide down that slippery road to glaring sin. Little compromises lead to bigger and bigger compromises. Small idols lead to larger ones.

Notice today what small idols your kid bows to. If you overlook seemingly insignificant acts of disobedience now, don't expect your child to exercise self-control and obedience when he's grown. Here are a few things to look for:

inconsistent church attendance
inconsistent prayer life
unforgiving and ungrateful spirit
rebellious, sullen attitudes
lack of respect for your standards
inconsistent grades, class attendance
experimenting with drug or alcohol use
use of bad language.

These behaviors reveal deeper attitudes toward God, authority, and what your child considers fun. They reflect attitudes as much as specific acts of disobedience do. They are attitudes that lead to behaviors like lying, smoking, cursing, telling dirty jokes, tolerating racist remarks, or weakening sexual standards. It all starts with a little compromise here and there.

Help your teen understand what a commitment "not to bow" means by understanding the gravity and reality of the story of Shadrach, Meshach, and Abed-Nego. "I will not bow" is a resolution to make before leaving home for school, work, or summer camp.

(Don't leave home without it.) If your child determines not to bow to the idols of the world, he's a long way toward standing for godliness. But if the resolution isn't made in advance, it won't be kept in the end. When he feels the heat of the fiery furnace, it's usually too late to make that commitment.

Your loving, godly support is the most important foundation for making this resolution part of your kid's life. Have your child list idols to which she resolves to say, "I will not bow." Talk about her list, and discuss ways she can resist these temptations and stand for God. A decision to stand against peer fear sticks best when it's accompanied by predetermined answers to tough situations.

3. GIVE YOUR KIDS OPPORTUNITIES TO START OVER

One night after church a neatly dressed fifteen-year-old girl came up to speak to me. She was a cute kid with long black hair, and it was obvious she'd been crying. She had my daughter's innocent face and puppy-dog eyes.

For about five minutes, between squalls of tears and numerous nose wipes, she told me how evil her parents were. They didn't like her friends, wouldn't let her talk on the phone or hang out. When I asked if she'd talked to them about her concerns, she said all they did was yell at her.

As I listened to this apparently horrible story of child abuse, I began to feel sorry for her; then a voice representing all the parents in the world smacked me in back of my head. "Boy, are you crazy?" it said. "Ask this girl what she did to deserve this treatment!"

I came to my senses. And asked. She responded without hesitation, those big eyes looking so sweet and innocent, "Nothing!"

Now I knew something was fishy, and the more we talked she admitted abusing her phone privileges, sneaking out late at night, and failing in her classes. The whole situation was a mess. She had definitely used up all her benefits, and her parents were worn out. But she was also being driven away by constant suspicion, and no one was benefiting from anything.

That family needed to sit down and declare a truce. Sometimes you need to hold out an olive branch of grace and give your kids and the relationship a chance to start over. Change the language of your negotiations. Don't forget to include words of love, hope, and grace in your contract. Bring in a counselor or other third party, if necessary, to work through your differences.

You might *know* you are right about your kid. Maybe you resent the way you've been worn down and worn out. But the most important issue isn't proving you're right. The most important goal is to get your child safely through this tumultuous time of life.

You don't need to compromise your values or standards, and you still may need to be tough. But don't lose the kid in the process. Sweeten your standards with grace, just as God does for you.

4. DEVELOP POSITIVE RELATIONSHIPS WITH YOUR KID'S FRIENDS

Your child will be impacted by the relationships you develop with his friends.

I conducted a chapel service for my children's class. When it was over, several kids wanted my autograph. They ran and got pens and papers, then gathered around waiting for me to sign my name. I have gotten used to signing autographs because of my football background, but when my kids saw their friends pushing each other to get to me, they wondered, *Just who is my dad?* Then they began fighting for position to be near me and tell everyone else, "He's my dad!" They even asked for my autograph!

You don't need to be famous in the eyes of your children's friends to be someone special. It doesn't take money or status to be kind, considerate, loving, and interested. When it comes to influencing young people, minor name recognition is nothing compared to being a good role model.

A few suggestions for getting to know your kid's peers:

- Show interest in their college and career choices.

- Set an extra plate at the dinner table when they're around and let them know they're welcome. Dinnertime is a good time for conversation.
- Acknowledge achievements in academics, sports, or the community.
- Spend quality time talking with them.
- Ask about family members by name.
- Always say hello, thank-you, please, sorry.
- Include them in some of your family activities.
- Notice new clothes or hairdos. (And say something creatively positive about the clothes and hair don'ts.)
- Offer to help find jobs, mentors, rides to church or school functions.

Regular contact and involvement in the lives of your kid's friends will accomplish several things:

- It gives your child a check on who his/her friends are and what they are about.
- It helps you sympathize with your child's friends instead of falsely judging them as someone not good enough for your kid.
- It gives those friends a sense of accountability for their behavior when they're with your kid.
- It helps you and your child minister to them more effectively.

Some of your children's friends are innocent victims of incredibly dysfunctional families. They need your love. Many don't know God, or have never tasted God's forgiveness. They are crying out for His love, and for the love of someone who knows God. Invite them to your home and intentionally care for them.

- Offer them rides to church.
- Invite them to special concerts and outreaches.
- Ask them how you can pray for them and their family's needs.
- Pray for them often, especially when they are present.
- Share your faith with them.

- Give them videos or CDs that will help them glimpse God.
- Be ready to listen if they need to talk to someone.
- Offer to direct them or their family to counselors, job opportunities, other resources.

Showing Christ's love to your child's friends is a tremendous ministry opportunity for you and your child. It's a concrete way to teach your child to share his faith in a loving, practical way.

5. TEACH YOUR KIDS TO PICK GOOD FRIENDS BY TEACHING THEM TO BE GOOD FRIENDS

Proverbs 18:24 says, "A man who has friends must himself be friendly."

Throughout their trial by fire, Shadrach, Meshach, and Abed-Nego never left one another's sides. They held each other up. Even when the fire raged and they believed they would die, they resisted evil together.

Challenge your child to share her faith with her friends and to seek out friends who will hold her spiritually accountable. Take time to discuss what is and isn't a healthy friendship. Remember, discussion implies you will listen as well as speak. Listen to your children's ideas, then share yours. Remind them that "evil company corrupts good habits" (1 Corinthians 15:33).

6. TEACH YOUR KID TO BE THE BEST OF FRIENDS

One night when I was seventeen, my friends and I went to the beach to hang out. We decided to race in the sand without shoes on. Suddenly something jabbed my foot. I looked down to see blood spurting onto the sand and realized I had been badly cut. One friend rushed me to the hospital. Two hours later I hobbled out on crutches, sporting ten stitches and a huge bandage. That same friend continued to drive me wherever I needed to go while my foot healed. I won't forget his friendship because in my time of need he was there.

Proverbs says that "a friend loves at all times" (17:17) and that "there is a friend who sticks closer than a brother" (18:24).

Discuss the meaning of friendship with your son or daughter. True friends hold each other accountable, challenge each other when one is straying, and remain loyal to one another through any ordeal. Challenge your child to evaluate his friends honestly so he can pray for their growth, know how to interact, and discern whether or not they should be hanging out together.

DON'T BOW
SURVIVING THE FIRE

Shadrach, Meshach, and Abed-Nego were teenagers, no more special than your kids or mine. They had plenty of reasons to be bitter, to turn on God, and to give in to the world system. But the right kind of peer pressure and a committed faith gave them the courage to say, "I will not bow."

They stood for God, even in the presence of the world's most powerful king. They knew that living isn't bowing down to gangs, but standing for righteousness. Living isn't bowing down to the crowd, but being used by the Holy Spirit to challenge the crowd. Living is telling the social bullies of the schoolyards and the world, "I won't bow to anyone but God." Living is having no fear of man, who can kill the body but not the soul. Living is leading life to impress God.

CHAPTER EIGHT

DESTINED TO...
BE PURE

> "Blessed are the pure in heart, for they shall see God."
>
> MATTHEW 5:8

"No one ever loses their virginity," I told the girls sitting on the wall at lunchtime. They gave me a puzzled, embarrassed look.

I continued, "When was the last time you heard someone walking through the halls yelling, 'Hey dude, have you seen my virginity? I lost it somewhere.'? No, you don't lose your virginity. Unless you've been raped, you give it away."

They were quiet, listening expectantly for me to say more. I had just finished speaking at their school when I spotted this group of students sitting on the privileged senior wall. I laughed to myself as I watched the too-typical interaction. Guys tossed their lines at the girls, thinking they were so smooth. The girls rolled their eyes and giggled.

I walked over and struck up a conversation. The girls knew I am a youth pastor, so I started asking questions that led to a discussion about sexual morality. I got their attention with the virginity line, but went on to tell them that sex is more than kissing and hugging.

Sex is about becoming one with someone. When you are married in the eyes of God, I told them, you are united as one, spiritually and emotionally, and sex is a wonderful physical symbol of that oneness.

"If you aren't joined as one by God, and you indulge in a union of the flesh, you end up losing a part of your soul," I concluded.

They sat spellbound, letting God's Word sink in. I watched how seriously they were listening. Suddenly one girl grabbed my arm, dragged me over to another friend and said, "You have to listen to this guy. He told us why we shouldn't have sex."

This wasn't the first time I had encountered teenagers looking for a reason *not* to be sexually active. They wanted to abstain. They instinctively knew premarital sex wasn't right or healthy, but no one had ever given them a good reason to say no.

I've discovered that in spite of the sexual revolution, many young people want to be sexually pure. Many are burdened by expectations put on them at a young age to be sexually active. Our young people want tools to battle temptation, resist social pressure, and protect themselves by abstaining.

BRAINWASHING

WHAT IS NORMAL?

"What's normal?" I get that question a lot from kids. Or "What's okay?" They want to know how far they're allowed to go and still feel some self-respect. I've had kids say to me, "I don't want to be a pervert." Young people have a great fear of being weird or abnormal or out of bounds, but they are confused. The problem is that "normal" and "okay" and "perverted" get redefined daily, especially by the media.

According to a national poll conducted by Children Now, a children's advocacy group, 62 percent of kids ages ten to sixteen said sex on TV influences children to engage in sex when they are too young. That's *kids* saying that, not the parents.

A *USA Weekend* survey of more than sixty-five thousand TV viewers revealed that 96 percent are very or somewhat concerned about the sex being portrayed on TV.

The American Family Association, whose research shows that 89 percent of all sex depicted on television occurs outside of marriage, states, "Heavy exposure to prime-time television programming featuring intimacy between unmarried persons can clearly result in altered moral judgments."

In countless prime-time TV programs, a couple meets, falls in love, makes love, gets engaged, breaks up, bounces back from the pain, and falls in love again, all within thirty or sixty minutes, and all with relatively few consequences. This scenario is especially common in shows targeted at young people, like *Beverly Hills 90210* and *Melrose Place*. What an unrealistic picture of life our young people get when heartbreaks are harmless, sexually transmitted diseases are disarmed, and having sex with someone is as casual as saying hello.

These startling statistics from the Center for Disease Control and other sources give us a pretty good idea of where our societal shift toward promiscuity has taken us:

- Forty percent of all teens are sexually active.
- Three million teenagers every year are diagnosed with a sexually transmitted disease.
- Sixty-three percent of all sexually transmitted diseases are reported among teenagers.
- Since the push for "safe" sex and condom distribution, the teenage birth rate has increased by 14 percent.
- The nation's first high school to adopt a condom distribution program for its students—in Denver, Colorado—has seen a 31 percent increase in the teenage birth rate.
- The number of abortions performed on teenagers has increased to almost one million per year.

The fashion industry fuels the fire with clothes designed to enhance the sexuality of young people. So great is the pressure to obtain a certain sexual look that older girls routinely consider breast implants. And little girls want push-up bras, even when there's nothing there to push up.

Scanning through popular music stations can be a shocking, almost X-rated experience. Graphic portrayals of abusive and immoral sexual behavior are common.

As I survey society, I can only conclude there is an insidious plan to brainwash our kids. If that sounds overly dramatic, look around and witness the damage. Destructive, abusive lifestyles are pushing more kids into depression and suicide than at any time in our nation's history. To many, purity is an elusive goal darkened by the stain of sin and regret.

HIGHER CHALLENGE

NOT TOO PROUD TO BEG

I've been speaking to kids long enough to have seen a few changes in teenage behavior—noticeably, among girls. I'm surprised at how often I'm approached by young girls with ridiculous propositions—not only in front of friends, but in huge assemblies.

A lot of this is just kids playing around, but I nevertheless find the boldness of these girls alarming. They have no shame, and so little self-respect. As the father of two daughters, I want to scold these girls and tell them how much they are harming themselves.

I challenge them back with the fact that I'm married and wouldn't consider breaking my marriage vows. Some of them have no clue! They don't comprehend the concept of commitment and working on a relationship. Most of these young people are so far from the level of maturity that makes a relationship work that I'm beginning to understand why the divorce rate is so high in this country. If young people "falling in love" bring these deficiencies into marriage, there's little hope for a meaningful family life.

One girl yelled out in front of her friends that she wasn't too proud to beg, a line that's the title of a song about a girl who doesn't mind begging for sex. I explained that a person gets to that point by being so sexually active and giving so much of him or herself away that there isn't much of a self left to be proud of.

Kids are more well informed about the risks of promiscuous sex than ever, yet that knowledge hardly seems to be slowing them down. During the filming of a video on abstinence, I interviewed about a hundred teenagers. On film, I ask kids to tell me about the dangers of sex before marriage in four areas: emotional, mental, social, and physical. Here are some of their responses:

- *Emotional dangers:* heartbreak, depression, suicidal tendencies, jealousy, envy
- *Mental dangers:* negative view of the opposite sex, bad memories
- *Social dangers:* bad reputation, friends with evil intentions, losing good friendships
- *Physical dangers:* Sexually transmitted diseases and tragic results, unwanted pregnancies

The one that takes the prize is the guy in Philadelphia who said you can be physically hurt from sex—when the girl's father beats you with a baseball bat. I bet this kid could run really fast!

Even knowing these dangers, kids engage in sexual behavior that is harmful and ultimately unsatisfying.

SKEWED VALUES

SEX RULES!

I was in Brooklyn, but there were no Dodgers, crowded streets, or New York accents. I was in Brooklyn, Michigan, a small town just outside of Detroit, conducting a class on abstinence. A traffic light or two, one junior high, and one high school—that was it, and I had all those kids as a captive audience.

I woke them up when I announced, "I want to teach you to have good sex—no, GREAT sex." They all started shouting and screaming, like I knew they would. The teachers were in a panic, but I knew I'd have them on my side in a minute.

"Tell me," I began, "are there rules to sex?"

They all started shouting things like, "No . . . just go with the

DESTINED TO . . . **BE PURE**

flow . . . do whatever you want. . . ."

"If there are no rules, can I have sex with my daughter?" The mood of the room changed abruptly. I knew it hit close to home for some kids. Then they yelled, "No, no . . . that would be wrong."

"I thought you said there were no rules," I responded. "Can I have sex with another man's wife?"

"No," they answered. "That would break up the family," one girl added.

"Can I have sex with another man?"

"Well, you could," one guy said. "But that would be nasty." The rest nodded in agreement.

Now that they were thinking, I told them these things can't just be wrong to be wrong. They're wrong because God says so. I explained that God made us with sexual desires, but He also gave us guidelines for fulfilling those desires within a healthy, meaningful relationship.

They were all listening now. I finished by telling them what I tell every kid every chance I get—that God created and designed sex like everything else. There are rules and guidelines given for our benefit, and those rules are found in the Bible. God's requirement is still sexual purity. When God said fornicators will not inherit the kingdom of God, He meant it. When He said Sodomites, homosexuals, adulterers, and the immoral will not inherit the kingdom of God, He meant it. In spite of our culture's disregard for moral goodness, God's standards haven't changed. But neither has His ability to equip young people with the tools to be pure no matter what the temptation.

The Bible's guidelines exist to protect us and our children from the worst kind of sin we can commit against our own bodies—sexual sin. The Bible tells us that when we are one with someone outside of marriage, it's like uniting the members of Christ to a prostitute (1 Corinthians 6:15).

The effect these statements have on kids is indescribable. I usually see tears, and in spite of a little macho kidding around, most of them get quiet and thoughtful. What I see in their faces is a hunger to be pure, and a fear that it isn't possible.

That's when—as much as I can get away with—I tell them about the power of God's love to renew them and give them a fresh, pure start. Sometimes I have to wait till an after-school pizza party, where I can be short, sweet, and straight to the point about the Gospel and the change for good God wants to make in their lives.

EXAMPLES TO FOLLOW

THE RULES DON'T CHANGE

At a sexual purity conference in an Ohio school, I mentioned that my wife and I had experienced two unplanned pregnancies, resulting in our second and third children.

A girl in the crowd jumped right on that one. "Oooh . . . see?! You're no different than us. You had a baby when you weren't planning to, just like us."

I pointed out the huge difference. My children have a mother and father who live together, love each other, and are committed to a lifetime of raising their children together. Sexual purity isn't a matter of just avoiding getting pregnant or catching a disease. It's a matter of conducting your sexual life within the guidelines set up by God. And that applies before and during marriage, before and after pregnancy.

Some people think that once they have fallen in love or are pregnant or get engaged, the rules change. But that's not what the Bible says, and those aren't the examples Scripture shows us.

Consider this scenario: A teenage girl, engaged to be married to an older man, is pregnant by someone other than her fiancé. That was Mary, the mother of Jesus. In spite of her unusual circumstances, her commitment to faith and purity was so strong that even though she was engaged and pregnant, she abstained from sexual relations with Joseph until they were officially married. Even then, she waited until after Jesus was born.

Another Joseph, the handsome, powerful young man and special assistant to Potiphar, ruler of Egypt, faced one of the most blatant attempts at sexual seduction recorded in the Bible. Potiphar's wife, "cast longing eyes on Joseph," Genesis 39 tells us. When he refused her advances, she started pulling his clothes off! Joseph did what any young person needs to do in the face of such temptation: he ran! ("Flee sexual immorality," 1 Corinthians 6:18).

Plenty of Christian young people think any guy or girl who seems semi-respectable is a viable candidate for a guy/girl relationship. They think they can lure a non-Christian into God's kingdom. They'll be friends, they'll fall in love, then their unbelieving boyfriend or girlfriend will suddenly fall for God. Again, God has an unchanging rule on "missionary dating." His Word tells us, "Do not be unequally yoked together with unbelievers. . . . For what communion has light with darkness?" (2 Corinthians 6:14).

In Genesis 24:3, Abraham the patriarch knew it was time to find a wife for his son Isaac. As the custom was, he sent his most trusted servant in search of the right candidate. Before the servant embarked, however, Abraham made him swear, ". . . by the Lord, the God of heaven and the God of the earth, that you will not take a wife for my son from the daughters of the Canaanites. . . ." Abraham knew that a wife with a foreign belief system would do nothing but cause a divided heart in his son.

CLEAR STANDARDS
PARENTS, ARE YOU READY?

A few years ago some friends gave my daughters the African-American Ken and Barbie dolls. Ken had a Jheri curl and a pretty good build (nothing like her dad, though). I think Barbie had hair extensions, but I'm not a gossip, so I'll never tell.

One day my four-year-old daughter grabbed Ken and said, "Dad, this is my man!"

Well, I was a little hurt. Even a little jealous. I thought, I am your man. After all, I'm the one who feeds you, encourages you, prays for you, buys your clothes, dreams for your best. Can this ten-inch plastic brother do any of those things? He doesn't even have a job.

I know the day will come when my daughters marry. I will teach them that when they do that it's time to leave their parents and cleave to their husbands. But in the meantime, I thought, as long as you live under my roof, I am your man. I was tempted to sneak into the toy box that night and dismember Ken.

My emotions caused me to stop and reflect. What will I do when a real Ken comes knocking on our door? What will *you* do when a member of the opposite sex has designs on your child? Are you ready and prayed up? *Before* your child gets interested in guy/girl relationships, ask yourself the following questions. Or, if they're already there, make sure you have these questions settled:

Have you set clear standards for your child's development of relationships with the opposite sex? Three considerations: The guidelines have to work for you; they have to be tolerable to your child; and they have to be rooted in God's ultimate wisdom as expressed in the Bible. This is a bigger issue than planning that your child won't date until she's thirty-five. We're all agreed on that. Actually, you can be thinking now of how to handle the real-life issues that will inevitably arise.

Start by praying now for your son's or daughter's mate, regardless of how young your child is. Then mull answers for these:

- Do you have an age requirement for your child for a serious relationship or for seeing one person exclusively? Or do you allow that at all? (Not at all is a great option, if your child is a young teen.)
- Do you have an age requirement for the person with whom your teenager pursues a relationship?
- Have you set down conditions, such as requiring the young man to come into the house, to meet you, the parents, or to simply say hello on subsequent occasions? (And to fill out an application complete with references from his pastor, his parents, and the FBI? Oh yeah, and to see the baseball bat!)

Maybe that last one is a bit extreme, but you get the idea.

One area where most parents need to do some solid thinking is the issue of interracial relationships. It's an area where parents often exhibit knee-jerk reactions they later regret.

One of the white teenage girls in our youth group wanted to start spending time with an African-American guy. Her parents had a big problem with that. When we met, at the girl's request, they explained that one of their concerns was that so many of the African-American kids come from broken homes.

We discussed the fact that most sociologists and marriage counselors agree that if interracial relationships lead to marriage, that couple will be hindered more by differences in faith and values than by the color of their skin. So rather than using race as a criteria, faith should be the common value that matters.

Have you discussed the true meaning of love with your kids? Since so many guys use the "If you love me . . ." line, it's important to define real love for your daughters—and your sons, in case they're ever tempted to use it, or some girl tries it on them.

I tell girls that we are to "love the Lord your God with all your heart, with all your soul, and with all your mind. . . . And . . . love your neighbor as yourself" (Matthew 22:37, 39). Then I tell them that 1 John 5:3 says that if we love God, we keep His commandments. So, if you want God's best, you need to love God, which means keeping His commandments.

And so here's the true-love test. When a girl tells me, "He loves me," I ask, "Does he help you obey God?" I fill that out: "Is his love encouraging you to read the Bible, pray, identify and develop your spiritual gifts? If he loves you God's way, he will encourage godliness. If he "loves" you Satan's way, you'll end up sinning."

That may sound wacko to you or your child or the person wanting to spend time with your child. But that's what God wants for His kids. If someone wants to date your teen, the number one question you need to ask isn't about race, age, or family background, but this: Is this person equipped to invest spiritually in your child's life?

Are you setting a godly example? With over half the marriages in this country ending in divorce, plenty of parents struggle with the same issues as their kids do. Knowing what the Bible says about purity is one thing. Living it is another. Your kids are watching you—trust me—and they will grab any excuse they can find to justify an excess of the flesh.

If you are single and dating, you need to abide by the same rules you lay down for your kids, no matter how old or mature you are: No sex outside of marriage. Date only believers. Be careful not to place yourself in a compromising situation. You cannot preach abstinence and practice fornication.

If you are married, your relationship with your spouse should be something your kids will watch and want to emulate: A husband who washes his wife with the water of God's Word. Mutual respect and consideration. A husband who loves his wife and cares for her as he would his own body. A couple passionately in love with each other. Frequent embraces. Heartfelt "I love you's."

Remember, the parents of a large number of your kids' friends are likely divorced. Those kids are trying to figure out what the whole marriage scene is about. Show them a living, biblical example of marriage. If you're single, let them see you committed to godly standards.

GIVE GUIDELINES

EQUIPPING FOR PURITY

Sexual purity rarely comes about on its own. The most powerful ally of sexual purity is well-developed, all-around godliness. But even people who love the Lord can fall (as we see throughout the Bible; e.g., King David and King Solomon). A few tools of wisdom help strengthen the resistance:

1. WATCH YOUR KIDS WITH WIDE-OPEN EYES

Parents, it's not time to *think* you know where your children stand on moral issues. It's time to *know*. What reputation does your child have? If someone uncovered the truth of his or her sexual behavior, what would it be? Do you know? Do you want to know? It's scary but necessary information.

Several years ago I held a Bible study at our home. About twenty-five young people of about nine nationalities came regularly. It was like a mini–United Nations.

Four girls always arrived together. One was Filipino, one Chinese, another Japanese, and the fourth a combination of all three. One girl really stood out from the others. Three of the girls were dressed to kill, hair sprayed up to the ceiling, leather pumps, and stretch pants. But Diane was different. She dressed modestly. Week after week I noticed she had a sincere interest in spiritual things. She accepted the Lord on her first visit and made a commitment to one-on-one discipleship soon after.

I asked a teenage guy from the neighborhood about her. He wasn't a Christian, and, as a matter of fact, he didn't like me too much at the time.

"She's a good girl," he said sarcastically, answering my question. I asked him what he meant. He said she "didn't put out." Just as I thought. She had a reputation as "good"—because she was!

Perhaps you don't really know your child's reputation. There are creative ways to find out, but I think the direct approach is best. Ask. Find out what he or she thinks about premarital sex. Divorce. Abortion. The truth may be painful, but in the end truth will set your child free, as you are able to confront, minister, and pray for healing.

2. USE YOUR SENSE OF SMELL

I encourage you to use the sniffalizer test, or "smell ya later." You might think I'm joking, but I'm not. Your sense of smell is one of your most useful tools in staying informed about your child's life.

Let me warn you. Technique and timing are crucial. And don't snort. I've known parents who did, got caught, and it was a mess. Close your mouth and inhale gently through the nostrils.

When your teenager comes home from a social evening, greet her with a hug.

The first sniff happens on your way into the hug. This is the breath check. You're sniffing for signs of alcohol, cigarettes, or marijuana.

During the hug, sniff around the hair, neck, and shoulder area. You're smelling for the above plus foreign cologne or maybe even car exhaust.

Take your last sniff as you pull away from the hug. This is to double-check the breath (she might clamp her mouth shut the first time, being wise to you, but by now she's had to take a breath).

Don't forget to make eye contact. Ask about the evening and make her look you in the eye.

"Smell ya later" will familiarize you with your kid's activities. Don't be surprised if you recognize the source of that foreign cologne one day when it walks through the door!

3. PASS THE ANIMAL REPELLENT

One day Laura walked into our youth service with a discouraged look on her face. I asked what was wrong, and, like most teenagers, she responded, "Nothing." Eventually she said, "Miles, I didn't get asked to the church semi-formal."

"No one asked you?"

"Well," she said, "one guy . . . but you know." She made a face.

I told her to look around the room and said, "There is no one here good enough for you." I meant it. She was more emotionally and spiritually mature than any of the guys in our group.

I told her one day God would bring along the right man who would sweep her off her feet and be her perfect mate. She needed to be patient and use the discernment God had given her.

Discernment gives young people what I like to call "animal repellent." It equips your child to defend herself.

When I was in high school there were two girls I wanted to meet. They weren't necessarily the prettiest girls in the school, but there was something about them I found irresistibly attractive. All through high school I tried to get up the nerve to approach one of them, but whenever I got close, something inside me said, "Back off, chump." I couldn't figure it out!

I never did meet them, but later I found out they were both Christians and virgins. I'm now convinced that it was their holiness and the power of God that kept me at a distance. I wasn't walking with the Lord then and had no good thoughts in me! Those girls were gifted with animal repellent.

4. REDEFINE DATING

One of the stickiest situations I faced as a youth pastor was deciding what to do when kids in the group wanted to start seeing members of the opposite sex on a regular basis. It was obvious. I'd be up teaching and could see them scoping the room, checking each other out, trying to figure out how to meet the cute guy or girl sitting on the other side.

I approached it two ways. First, I told them we were going to redefine dating. The Song of Solomon says, "Do not stir up or awaken love until it pleases" (2:7). Once young people are exposed to sexual practices, they will be affected for life. It's hard to go back. The flesh has experienced the sensation, the mind has processed the information, and the heart understands lust and how to entertain thoughts of it. Until the time is right, don't pour gas on the fires of love!

To have a successful relationship doesn't mean to have a physical encounter, I tell them. Quite the contrary. Redefine the whole concept. Build friendships, hang out together in groups, don't pair off with one individual. Slow down the whole process. Keep the focus on spiritual things. Pray, study the Bible, and do ministry together.

Second, we set up an "accountability outing" ministry. We paired teen couples with adult couples. My wife and I went out regularly with several young couples. Two of them will be married this year. We helped them shape their relationships by being role models and being open in our discussions. They learned to behave together, and they knew when they saw me I was going to ask them hard questions like, "Are you being tempted? Are you struggling? Have you sinned? Gone too far? Is he or she pushing you?"

Help your kids establish a relationship with an adult or peer who will hold them accountable and ask the tough questions.

Mr. "T" once said, "I pity the fool who wants to date my daughters. I feel even more sorry for the girls who want to date my son, because they'll have to deal with my wife. We tell them no kissing, no talking, no touching, and never even look at each other. Be home in fifteen minutes."

Again, a little extreme, but the idea is accountability—for the protection of our kids.

Third, make sure this significant other is prepared and committed to loving your child—helping them to obey God. This means encouraging obedience to God while on their so-called date—where they are always accompanied by others—as well as nurturing your child's overall spiritual growth.

5. DEFINE "TOO FAR"

Kids ask me all the time how far is "too far." One day on a high school campus, a girl came up to me and asked if it was okay to tongue kiss with her boyfriend. I answered her with another question. "When you're through kissing, are your clothes still on?"

She breathed an exasperated sigh, flung her hair back, and walked off. Two months later she was pregnant, by a boyfriend who left her.

I tell young people they can do anything they want—as long as it does not cause them to lust in their hearts. Matthew 5:28 tells us, "Whoever looks at a woman to lust for her has already committed adultery with her in his heart." Author Ed Cole puts it this way: "Lust desires to please self at the expense of others because lust wants to get. Love desires to please others at the expense of self because love wants to give."

I ask young people to measure their relationships and behaviors against that statement. Is the other person selfishly lusting after you, or is he willing to trade his selfish desires for what is best for you? I also tell them that instead of asking how close to the fire they can get without getting burned, they should ask themselves how close to God's holiness they can get.

While your kids are young, start speaking honestly and openly about these things. They need to determine in advance how far is too far to avoid sexual traps later.

6. ERR ON THE CONSERVATIVE SIDE

I was with some friends at a restaurant when their daughter walked in, dressed in skimpy little shorts and a tank top. I teased her about attracting the wrong kinds of guys, and she responded in a squeaky little voice, "Oh, there's nothing to worry about."

Her mother, feeling a little defensive, said something about her daughter only dressing that way around them, because she felt safe. I thought, *Don't kid yourself.*

While each family has to decide what works for them, I encourage you to err on the conservative side. Be a little more careful than you think you need to be. Parents, if you saw someone else's kids looking or acting like yours, what would you think? I hear parents gossip about the children of friends or colleagues—yet they would never judge their own kids by the same measure. Do you acknowledge that your young angel has desires?

7. TEACH ESCAPE ROUTES

When a girl feels she is in danger of being taken advantage of, she needs to know there are escape routes. Teach her how to get out of a bad situation—and the same applies to guys. You can enroll your kid in a self-defense course, but, whatever you do, communicate three simple rules:

1. *Don't worry about hurting feelings.* Never worry about hurting someone's feelings in a situation like this. When you say NO, say it loud and clear and don't be intimidated into changing your mind.

Potiphar's wife was offended when Joseph rejected her—enough to have him thrown in jail. He still did the right thing and was rewarded later.

2. *Defend yourself.* If necessary, run, yell, scream, fight, punch . . . you are allowed to protect yourself. If you get out of the car, don't get back in.

3. *Always have a backup plan.* Carry money for a phone call, cab, bus, whatever. If affordable, a cell phone is a good idea. Come to think of it, going out with other couples in the first place is an even better idea. Avoid being alone at all costs.

8. DON'T BE FOOLED

A committed and conscientious Christian family has a beautiful daughter, the object of many a young man's desire. From an early age, she had been taught right from wrong and, when she turned sixteen, was given strict dating guidelines. She complied with them easily and all was well—until she met Mr. Perfect. Only seventeen, he epitomized the "super Christian boyfriend," also from a committed and conscientious family.

Neither set of parents thought these kids would fall. They had been taught well, and their parents trusted them. Unfortunately, they were young and everyone was a little too confident. As a result, their parents didn't monitor their activities closely, and they got in way over their heads.

The relationship fell apart. Both felt guilty about their sexual experimentation, and both were too young to make a mature commitment. When they broke up, their lives went into a tailspin, each consumed with heartache and guilt.

Nothing can save any of us from the angst of young love, but it can be tempered with godly wisdom. Parents, keep a close watch on your kids. Give them curfews and help them be accountable for their activities in the ways we have discussed. Never assume too much.

None of us is superhuman. "Let him who thinks he stands take heed lest he fall," 1 Corinthians 10:12 warns us.

SECOND CHANCE

FORGIVENESS, MERCY, AND REDEMPTION

Even if you have applied every principle ever written on teenage sexuality, your young person can still fall. That doesn't make you or your child a failure. Neither is it the end of the world or the end of your son's or daughter's spiritual life.

While preaching during the first night of our Miles Ahead Crusade in San Diego, the Lord told me to say, "If you are a prostitute, God will forgive you of your sin." I thought to myself, *These are kids; there's no prostitute out there.* The Lord and I went back and forth as I rattled off other sins—drugs, stealing, lying, etc. I finally gave in and said, "If you are a prostitute tonight, God loves you and wants to forgive you." *That was dumb*, I thought. The next day I "happened" to call a friend who "happened" to have brought a sixteen-year-old prostitute who needed to hear those precious words. She became one of 2,560 teenagers who received God's forgiveness that weekend.

Our God is a God of forgiveness and second chances—and third . . . and fourth . . . While your child's actions may indeed have serious consequences, don't ever let him feel he can't come back to the Lord and find complete forgiveness, mercy, and redemption.

When Jesus taught the Beatitudes, He said, "Blessed are the pure in heart, for they shall see God." *Pure in heart* . . . because no one, not one of us, is pure in our flesh. We have all sinned and fallen short of the glory of God. We are all given the opportunity to come to God in repentance and to find forgiveness and mercy.

If you need to confront your son or daughter about sexual sin, be sure you provide an opportunity for confession and repentance. Let him know he can tell you the truth. Encourage him to go to anyone he has offended and seek forgiveness. Then lead him to prayer, reminding him of 1 John 1:9, "If we confess our sins, He is faithful and just to forgive us our sins and to cleanse us from all unrighteousness."

Remember, purity begins in the heart. Only then does it work its way out to the outer person. Confession, repentance, and forgiveness will purify your child's heart and allow him to once again see God.

DESTINED TO. . . .
LEAD

> " And a little child shall lead them. . . . "
>
> ISAIAH 11:6

Danny was in my face. I tried to step back, but he kept coming at me, bold and direct, with ideas spilling out of him. He was funny, too, and made me laugh until I finally had to hold up my hands to slow him down a little.

"Come on over here, away from the crowd," I said. I motioned him off to the side of the stage.

My first month as a youth pastor wasn't quite through, and I was still trying to get it all together. The service had just ended, and in my usual post-game analysis, I was disappointed. The night felt uneventful and flat. The worship sounded horrible, the pizza was giving me heartburn, and the crowd was small and indifferent. Now about forty young people stood jabbering about nothing. I stood looking at the kids and thinking discouraging thoughts, when all of a sudden there's Danny, talking as fast as a human mouth can move, three inches from my face.

I had no idea who the kid was, but I instantly liked him. He was the only live body in the room.

At first the sheer number of suggestions he threw out amused me. As I started to process what he said, I began to realize how right he was. He wanted to make our youth group more dynamic by starting a drama team to put on skits before the sermon. He brazenly said the worship team needed help and suggested letting kids take over. When I asked what instrument he played, he promised to start guitar lessons—now.

In mere weeks, Danny organized frequent skits and a new youth worship team—one that was eventually good enough to play for the entire adult church!

Danny had obvious creativity and courage. But he was also obviously a leader, evidenced by the number of people who followed him. He had the ability to draw together a group of people, get them excited about a common goal, and work with them to get there. Raised in a hardworking middle-class family, it was obvious Danny understood the concept of "just do it."

A leader isn't the loudest, boldest, or most creative person in the room. A leader is someone with a trail of people hustling after him. I tell kids, "If you're not being followed, you're just taking a walk."

Maybe you're figuring that everyone isn't cut out to be a leader, so this chapter probably won't apply to *your* kid. Stay tuned. Each of us, even in a small sphere of influence, has people who look at us as some kind of example. Every young person has the potential to lead. I dare you to notice the kids who already follow the example your child sets—again, even in a small way.

Each of us, then, has leadership skills to cultivate.

BLIND LEADING THE BLIND

LOST LEADERS

For a decade now sociologists have decried the loss of strong leadership for our youth. Thirty-five percent of today's youth can't identify any adults as heroes or role models for successful living. The problem isn't complicated. We don't have leaders because we don't develop leaders.

A DEARTH OF LEADERSHIP

Some of our communities' most dynamic leaders are involved in illegal or immoral activities. They know how to get people to step in line, but lack moral integrity. They lead where we don't want our kids to follow.

When a pizza delivery man was brutally murdered by a San Diego teenager nicknamed Bones, the story made national news. What was most shocking was the discovery that what started as a gang robbery only turned into murder after the gang leader yelled to Bones, "Get him!" Bones will spend the rest of his life in prison for following his leader.

If young people can be so easily influenced to kill, can't we provide opportunities to lead them into good?

Keeping kids busy and out of trouble is one thing, but giving them tools and opportunities to become problem solvers and leaders is another. In Escondido, California, citizens gathered in a town meeting to organize young leadership. Teenagers were picked from various local schools and asked to voice their opinions on youth violence and other issues. After the meeting, a fifteen-year-old girl summed up the next step. "I hope," she said, "that they will listen to what we said." Kids are eager to prove they can solve some of society's problems. It's great to let them talk. But we also need to give young people a chance to act.

FAMILY LEADERSHIP

We would like youth to lead. But why isn't it happening?

Families are the first incubator for leadership, but leadership training doesn't often happen at home. There are usually three reasons why:

1. Parents don't recognize leadership abilities in their children. We want kids to make wise decisions, and we know that one day they will handle responsibility—but we don't think it will happen while they are living at home. We tend to think children under our roof are followers. This is true to a point, but most youth are capable of more.

2. Parents let their egos get in the way. I've seen parents who feel threatened by a smart kid. They're afraid that if the kid is right, it means they are wrong. So they require their children to stand back and remain quiet, excluding them from adult conversation and sending the message: "Don't speak unless you are spoken to." While there is the element of children showing respect for their elders, children can have valuable opinions. If we only see them as uneducated and immature, a partnership to develop leadership will never form between us and our children.

3. Watching a child fail is hard. The risk of watching a child fail is too great for some parents. So they become overprotective. They are stressed at seeing their child take risks that will develop into leadership. To avoid the stress, they train their kids to avoid obstacles altogether rather than jump over them.

CHURCH LEADERSHIP

If the family is a child's first school of leadership, the church can be the greatest, where members of Christ's body gifted with leadership potential are nurtured, developed, and launched. Sadly, it doesn't happen often enough.

One component of spiritual leadership is spiritual maturity. It isn't biblical to give more responsibility to a person than that individual is ready to handle. But caution can cause us to miss the Spirit's leading. There are times when young people are mature enough to handle responsibility but aren't challenged to do so. Even when youthful leadership would be beneficial, young people—even in their twenties—are rarely sought out. Most opportunities to serve are reserved for adults.

This obviously isn't true in all churches. But when they overlook youth, they leave untapped one of their most valuable assets. Encourage your church to look for areas of service than can be as easily filled by a young person as an adult, and you will develop servant leaders. Give a teenager a vision of what it means to be a mature believer, and they will lead the future.

YOUNG LEADERS

A CHILD SHALL LEAD . . .

Israel had become a land where "the word of the Lord was rare . . . there was no revelation." Eli, the priest in office, had grown old and weary, heartsick over the sins of his sons. The land lacked strong spiritual leadership.

But God had a plan, and informed Eli, "I will raise up for Myself a faithful priest who shall do according to what is in My heart and in My mind. I will build him a sure house, and he shall walk before My anointed forever" (1 Samuel 2:35).

Meanwhile, young Samuel "grew in stature and in favor both with the Lord and men." He was the plan, chosen by God while still a boy to be the last king/priest of Israel before the offices were divided. Samuel's mentor, Eli, in spite of his troubles, recognized the calling and encouraged Samuel to obey.

Years later, when Samuel went in search of the future king of Israel, he didn't doubt God's anointing of another teen, David. He understood the potential of a young person anointed by God because he was young when he accepted God's call to lead.

In the book of Numbers we read that only men twenty years old and above were considered suitable for battle. But in chapter 3 we read that *all* children, one month and older, were to be numbered. In each tribe the children who were numbered were given responsibilities. For example, chapter 3, verse 25: "The duties of the children of Gershon . . . included the tabernacle, the tent with its covering, the screen for the door. . . ." Children of other families were assigned care of the ark, the tables, lampstands, and sacred utensils. The children were taught from an early age to take responsibility for important things. These were not token jobs. The ark was the most sacred of Israel's possessions.

Think back over the illustrations in this book of the many young people God called and used in amazing leadership positions. One I haven't mentioned yet is Gideon, a young man plucked from obscurity and thrust into leading his nation's armies.

Gideon was in hiding. Times were perilous. Israel's enemies had wiped out most of her resources and the army was exhausted. When an angel confronted Gideon, he responded, "O my lord, if the Lord is with us, why then has all this happened to us?" (Judges 6:13).

God simply replied, "Go in this might of yours, and you shall save Israel from the hand of the Midianites. Have I not sent you?" (6:14). Despite some false starts, Gideon obeyed the Lord and became his nation's hero.

There are two things I want to point out about Gideon's story—two things that all leaders need:

1. Gideon had faith. No one had ever done what he was about to do, and the task looked impossible. The first mark of a godly leader is the ability to venture into unknown territory. Without faith it is impossible to please God, Hebrews 11:6 tells us. It definitely takes faith to venture where no one has gone before. Being the first to do anything is scary, but when you realize that being first in man's eyes means being second to the power of God, you can do all things.

2. Gideon was supported and encouraged by his father. When God told Gideon to tear down the idols of his community, the entire town called for his death. His father defended him and stood by him, knowing his son couldn't handle that much pressure alone. His father realized that God himself had called his son to lead the nation, and that there was a price to pay for this privilege. His dad stood by his son's side while God prepared Gideon to be the leader He intended him to be.

Children need parents who will stand by them, defend them, and provide the environment for God to develop leadership qualities.

DOING YOUR BEST

THE BEST SELF

Do you look at your child and see a leader? Maybe you're just hoping the kid will survive adolescence. Any big, lofty dreams of leadership just don't compute.

You could be looking at the situation all wrong. Remember, a leader is simply someone who is followed. Leaders don't have to be followed by huge crowds. A leader might simply be leading one person at a time.

Leaders don't always have to be the winner or the best or the first in line. How many times have you thought, *My child must be first; must have the best grades; must be at the head of his class.* But that's not what makes a leader. If your child can follow Jesus down the road He has chosen for him, and do it with confidence, then others will follow.

It's a mistake to force your child into a mold that doesn't match his individual ability and personality, or God's call on his life. God created each individual uniquely and knows how He will use each one.

For example, we needed about twenty hours of video edited from one of our crusades. Sixteen-year-old Todd sat in a room for hours watching and editing all the footage down to two dynamic video pieces. He volunteered, made the commitment, then took charge and followed through on the job. He was content to be behind the scenes in production and didn't want a lot of attention for his efforts. He is an example of a quiet leader. He might never speak in front of a school assembly, but his example will certainly be followed by someone.

My point is this: Your child might not be the leader of the pack, or even come in second place, but that's okay. The goal of leadership is not being the best of all but being the best self.

As you think about how to develop leadership qualities in your children, ask yourself the following questions:

Are you blind to your child's leadership abilities because he

doesn't lead the way you think he should? To some, if leaders aren't up front, taking charge, talking loudly, ordering people around, or aggressively going after what they want, they aren't real leaders. Be patient. With the proper nurturing, your child will be as aggressive, up-front, or self-confident as God has designed him to be.

Do you recognize that leadership abilities require both training and failure? As any great leader can tell you, leadership has both costs and risks. A high level executive was assigned one of his bio-tech firm's largest accounts, involving a valued client and a $10 million asset for the company. Even though he was a fairly new employee, his boss had faith in him to work out the details and close the deal. After months of hard work, he lost the entire account—and, he figured, his job. He made an appointment with the company president to turn in his resignation and to thank him for the opportunity. To his surprise, the president refused to consider his resignation. In fact, he told him that he was going to be a valuable part of the company in years to come. "Besides," he said, "I just spent ten million dollars training you."

Take heart when you see your kids' failures. Consider them as training.

Has your child developed misguided leadership skills? Richard was the bully in a neighborhood full of bullies. He added to the violent nature of his 'hood by regularly beating up kids and smashing their faces into car windshields. He was clearly the established leader of the pack. The more I heard about him, the more I wanted to meet him. I figured if his direction could be changed it would influence a lot of other kids.

He was intimidating to meet at first. Well-built, with a black belt in karate, he had the muscle to, well, smash faces into car windshields. He also had an appealing personality, I discovered. In spite of the violence, he laughed a lot and made others feel good. We hit it off instantly, and one day he invited me to a party where there was supposed to be some trouble. By the time we got there, about a hundred kids had crowded around two teenagers getting ready to fight. I watched, amazed, as Richard plowed right through the crowd, grabbed the two kids and brought them over to me. I asked them what they were fighting about, and, as usual, it was nothing important. The whole situation was defused, to the disappointment of the crowd, and there was no fight.

Richard was clearly gifted with leadership skills. They were just misguided. Eventually he accepted the Lord and began to attend Bible study, and, just as I had hoped, many followed.

Just because your kid is in some kind of trouble, don't write off his leadership skills. Begin to pray today for God to redirect and challenge your child.

Are you willing to let your child pay the price of training? Leaders have a spirit of independence. They understand how their ship handles and aren't afraid to take it into uncharted waters.

Bruce grew up in a family with little money. His dad worked hard but could barely cover the family's basic needs. Bruce knew that if he was going to have the bicycle he wanted for Christmas, he would have to earn it. He knew that if he wanted a pair of sneakers, he was going to pay for them. At the age of seven he started his first business. By the time he was sixteen, he was employing three of his high school teachers for summer jobs. Today, he challenges his own kids to build their own businesses. He grew up believing, "I must, therefore I can." Do you believe your kid is capable of paying the price for maturing and developing into a leader? Or is your child always going to have you by her side doing everything for her?

Are you ready to give up "fix-it love" and develop "support love?" Fix-it love makes everything okay all the time so your kid can win. Unfortunately, it also creates an unrealistic balance between reality and opportunity. Your child gets conditioned to the mentality, *Mom or Dad will fix things so I can get what I want.* This isn't reality. Support love provides encouragement, guidance, wisdom, and your presence, when needed, to empower your child to go for it. When the day of battle comes, when she needs to stand strong during a crisis or test of faith, your child will be prepared to fight with the Lord at her side, rather than depending on Mom and Dad. Remember, you won't always be there. The sooner everyone learns that, the better.

If you believe that you must always fix your kid's problems— worse yet, if your kid believes you will always come running with a fix—she will never reach her leadership potential.

Do you believe that you are investing in one of tomorrow's leaders? Your child is someone who will make a difference in the world. If you don't believe, then I challenge you to change your way of thinking and believe in what God can do through your kid. Start praying today for the Lord to prepare your young person for leadership, then start watching for evidence of answered prayers.

LOOK FOR A LEADER

SIGNS OF LEADERSHIP

What is your child already doing that makes him or her a leader? While you might be looking for the obvious, it's time to pay attention to the more subtle characteristics of leadership and see if they are indeed operating within your child's life. After all, now that you've committed to praying for leadership qualities in your kids, you need to believe that God is answering. You don't want to miss the answer! There might also be things you *don't* see. By being aware, you can encourage your son or daughter to keep growing.

Has your child ventured into unknown territory? If there is one television show I can't bring myself to watch, it's *Star Trek*. I'm sorry, but I can't understand how they can put people on television with a crab on their face. Or expect us to take seriously characters with names like "Worf" or a race called "Klingon." My wife, on the other hand, is a mystery to me. I sometimes wonder how we ended up married. She is a total Trekkie.

There is one thing, however, that I really like about the show. It's the opening monologue where the captain describes their mission to "go where no man has gone before."

If you watch closely, you will see your child go places he's never gone before. It might even be a place you've never talked about or even thought of. You might find yourself watching in amazement as the young person before you attempts things or dreams of things unique to his or her personality.

Adam was in junior high when he did what no one before him had done. The teacher for sixth grade woodshop had an annual tradition. He set up a model business corporation with his students, complete with a manufacturing plant—to produce a woodshop item—and stocks. The students could invest in the business by buying stocks for fifty cents apiece. Then they sold their products, counted their profits, and made a little money on their investments.

Most kids bought three or four dollars worth of stocks. Well, Adam did a little research and found out that in the past, the students at least doubled their money every time. Having just had a birthday, he took that money and cleaned out his savings and ordered $150 in stocks. Since none of his students had ever attempted such a large investment, the teacher called Adam's parents to make sure they approved.

Adam not only doubled his money but became somewhat of a legend at his junior high. He saved every year to make his big investment, signing up for woodshop as often as he could. He got other kids motivated, and the little pretend business the teacher had set up turned into more of a real corporation with a lot of excited young entrepreneurs.

Adam's parents watched their normally shy son become a budding leader in the business world as he continued to start and operate his own businesses throughout his high school and college years. Today, at a young age, he is part of management for a large international company.

What positive things are they doing for the first time, without prompting from you? My second daughter, Kimmie, is always the first to clean up after herself. That wasn't always true. One day I realized that no one had to remind her; she just always got up from a meal or playtime and started picking things up. Other kids feel guilty enough to actually follow her lead. I call her "Captain Clean-up" (*not* after Captain Kirk!). Pay attention to the first time your child does similar things, like

saying thank-you

getting up when someone else needs a seat

asking for directions when confused or lost

helping someone who needs assistance

signing up for a club or team without prodding

taking charge of a meeting among peers

encouraging someone else

Some of these things might not seem like a big deal, but they are huge for kids. Notice them and encourage them. These small steps toward leadership will lead to bigger ones. Even simple things like saying "thank-you" set a good example that another kid will follow.

Is your child displaying godly traits you didn't think mattered to him? The other day on the playground at my kids' school I heard a little fourth grader stand up in a group of her friends and say, "I think we need to stop gossiping. It's just wrong and we're hurting each other's feelings." The other little kids all looked at her seriously and nodded as if to say, "Sure, that's right. Whatever you say." It was cute to watch, but I was also impressed with the leadership potential I saw in that little girl.

When you see your kid do something like that, let her know you're proud. Encourage her, and thank God for developing this area of your child's life. It takes guts for a young person to stand up for what she believes is right, and we need to support her when she does, just as Gideon's father stood by him.

Does your kid seize moments of opportunity in her areas of interest? Some young people automatically try out for a play as soon as sign-ups are announced, or stay after school to stand in line for a new activity. Other kids need a little coaxing and encouragement. Even if you have to go down and stand in line with your kid, help her take advantage of opportunities when you sense she wants to but is shy or intimidated. If you help her build self-confidence, eventually she'll do it on her own.

Is your child someone who figures out how to overcome obstacles in his own way? While I was watching the 1996 Olympics in Atlanta, I realized that Derrick Atkins, a runner in the 400-meter hurdles, graduated from my high school. He not only won his race, but did it with unique technique.

When a runner is in the starting block for a hurdles race, he can't see the finish line—only the hurdles. He knows from the beginning that there are obstacles to overcome, and he trains accordingly. The goal is to bolt over the obstacles faster than anyone else. Conventional training dictates that the runner get his lead foot onto the ground as fast as possible. Derrick, a mechanical engineer, figured out that if he could glide over the hurdle, thereby spending more time in the air, it would increase his speed. He proved his method by winning the gold medal.

Does your child exhibit boldness or courage? While preparing for our first Miles Ahead crusade in 1996, one school gave us a hard time about passing out flyers. The principal was against the Christian nature of our event, and accused us of violating separation of church and state precedents. No matter how legal he tried to make it sound, I knew he was the one breaking the law by preventing the Christian club the same access to the student body as the other clubs on campus had.

I explained the situation to Ty, one of the Christian students, telling him I could provide the necessary legal information if someone was willing to approach the principal. I wasn't sure how he would respond, but sooner than I could doubt his willingness, he answered, "It's done, no problem." He went to the principal and took care of it. His mother was proud of him but also pleasantly surprised. She had no idea he could be so bold.

How do other kids look at your kid? A sure sign of leadership potential is the way other kids view your child.

Ty was not only bold, but he was also a good role model. I noticed how other kids looked at him and followed his lead. He encouraged other students to attend church, read the Bible, and avoid temptation. Several parents expressed to me their appreciation of Ty's commitment and example.

Do you know what effect your son or daughter has on other kids? Ty's parents were surprised when I told them—like so many of us, they had no idea their son possessed such leadership qualities.

Does your child persistently ask questions? When that little four-year-old follows you around the house asking "Why?" and "What's this?" all the time, stop, take a deep breath, and pray for patience. It's cute at first, I know, but it can get wearying when it lasts twenty-four hours a day. I know a little kid who woke his parents up in the middle of the night to ask why it was dark. Kids with leadership qualities are inquisitive.

SEIZE THE OPPORTUNITY
LEADERS MAKE THE BEST OF A SITUATION

Leaders appear to be in the right place at the right time, getting all the breaks. But in reality, we are all in the right place at the right time if we take advantage of what is before us. A leader seizes the moment. She uses circumstances, education, job opportunities, even obstacles to her advantage.

Todd, the student who edited our video, had a neighbor who owned some of the most advanced digital editing equipment available. Todd asked so many questions and was so interested that his neighbor taught him how to work the equipment. At school, Todd took advantage of every opportunity to learn about audio/visual production. When it came time to edit our video, he showed up, committed himself to the project, and spent long hours editing and producing. He learned on the job.

It wasn't just good luck that helped Todd get so much training. It was his desire to learn from the situations around him. Today he is preparing to attend one of the best film production colleges in the country. I have no doubt he will emerge as a leader in the film industry.

THE BIG PICTURE

SEE YOUR CHILD FOR THE FIRST TIME

Obviously, there are many more qualities of leadership we could discuss—discipline, self-control, charisma, vision, purpose—many of the things we discussed in previous chapters. I picked out a few of the less obvious ones above to discuss because my prayer is that by the time you finish this chapter—this whole book—you are already starting to look at your child with fresh eyes.

Remember, when it comes to our kids, what we see isn't always what we get. Beneath that confused, sullen, insecure, hormonally-driven adolescent exterior, is a child of God with enormous potential. But we have trouble seeing our kids the way God sees them because we don't know the big picture. All we know is that we're trying to get through the week without a call from a teacher—or the police— or a big blowup or another thing to worry and pray about.

If you look at the list of signs of leadership and find yourself saying, "I don't read anything here that even remotely resembles my kid," don't be discouraged. God sees what's in the heart of your child. The leadership potential in young people isn't always obvious to adults. Adults ignored David, but God had a plan for David to be king. Through *His* power, it came to pass. He has a purpose for your child's life as well.

OPEN THE DOORS

BUILDING LEADERSHIP

Young people won't all be the same kinds of leaders. Some will lead the masses, others smaller groups, and some will lead only to themselves and a small sphere of influence, like an immediate family. Whatever the degree of leadership God anticipates for your child, there are ways you can help your kid fulfill his potential.

1. HELP YOUR CHILD MEET OTHER LEADERS

You can't legislate friendship, but you can arrange professional relationships. Your kids need examples of leadership in their lives. When you hear of someone who is progressing down a path that would benefit your kids, look for ways to connect them—lessons, tutoring, jobs, clubs. Be creative.

One dad watched his son become an avid surfer, and knew that there were some bad influences in the surf community, though good ones as well. The dad is a professional photographer, so he used his skill to connect his son to the good influences. He invited a bunch of kids from their church, including the older Christian surfers, to go on early morning surf patrols, while he photographed them. They loved that! They thought for sure they'd end up in *Surfer* magazine. His son made positive friendships in the surf community, and in turn went on to be a good example to other younger kids.

2. STEP OUT OF THE WAY

One day my family went for a hike in the mountains. We had no specific agenda or plan. My children kept asking, "Daddy, where are we going? What's ahead? When are we getting there?" I began to get irritated. I just wanted to walk, and they wanted some big plan! So I decided to put them up front, while I walked in the back and asked questions. I gave each child a chance to lead the hike, plan the way to go, and decide what our purpose was. I got out of the way and let them practice leadership.

Any time you give children a chance to be followed, you build leadership skills into them. Try these small things:

- Allow a child to pick a family activity.
- Allow a child to tell you how to drive home.
- Ask the children to plan a family vacation—giving them goals (sight-seeing, education, plain fun), a time frame, and budget parameters.
- Allow your child to plan a family dinner out—make the reser-

vations, order the food, figure the tip, and pay the bill (with your money, of course).

- Ask your child to give you a tour of his or her school.
- Let your child make class selections in older grades—gather all the information, make a decision, then present it to you for discussion.
- Give your child opportunities to speak in adult conversations—answering questions for his or herself as he or she learns to interact with adults.

GOD AT WORK

GOD IS IN CONTROL

Whenever I wonder how things are going to turn out for a kid, I think of Ryan.

The first time I saw him, he was sitting in the back of the youth group room on a Sunday morning. He had long, sandy brown hair, flowing past the shoulders of his leather jacket. He obviously didn't want to be there, but his brother was an adult leader and had convinced him to come. For most of his teen years, Ryan was moderately involved, at best, and his commitment to the Lord went up and down. He was initially excited about the Lord, then fell away for a time.

Ryan's brother believed in him, though. He was convinced Ryan would be a great leader and asked me to pray with him often about Ryan's commitment. To him, it was only a question of when the leader in Ryan would emerge.

Then Ryan discovered football. His love for the game gave him a passion for something he'd never had before. He put all of his energy into working out and qualifying for a football scholarship.

He made it to college, and everything changed. He solidified his commitment to Christ and soon became the spiritual leader of his team. He began leading Bible studies and challenging other players. I can't tell you how rewarding it was to read a newspaper article featuring Ryan and his unwavering commitment to the Lord. Finally, Ryan's life was properly aligned.

Some would argue about the *correctness* of this sequence of events. Some have said Ryan should have recognized *first* that God is a higher priority than football.

But God is in control. Ryan found football first, then Christ, and then he got his priorities right. That's the way it happened, and nothing can change that. Ryan's parents and family stayed positive. They never gave up on him. They kept praying and encouraging him until he emerged as a strong, passionate spiritual leader.

I want to end this chapter by sharing a wish for your children. I hope you will share it with them:

A Wish for Leaders

I sincerely wish that you will have the experience of thinking up a new idea, planning it, organizing it, following it to completion, and having it be magnificently successful. I also hope you go through the same process and have it "bomb out."

I wish you could achieve some great good for mankind, but have nobody know about it but you.

I wish you could find something so worthwhile that you deem it worthy of investing your life.

I hope you become frustrated and challenged enough that you begin to push back the very barriers of your own personal limitations.

I hope you make stupid mistakes and get caught red-handed and are big enough to say those magic words: I was wrong.

I hope you give so much of yourself that some days you wonder if it's worth all the effort.

I wish for you a magnificent obsession that will give you reason for living and purpose for life.

I wish for you the worst kind of criticism for everything

you do, because that makes you fight to achieve beyond what you normally would.

I wish for you the experience of leadership.

—Anonymous

CHAPTER TEN

DESTINED TO...
SHINE

> *Fan into flame the gift of God which is in you.*
>
> 2 TIMOTHY 1:6

I shivered in the hollow, worn-out auditorium. One of the coldest winters in history and I was in Rochester, New York, freezing and praying for the kids who would noisily spill into the room in a few minutes. A girl had been raped in this room just days before. I shuddered again, feeling the depression that chilled the school far below the dip on the thermometer.

Even so, after I prayed I felt confident God would prevail. We were going to have a good time that morning.

I do two things before every assembly, besides pray. First, I check out the environment and mood. Lighting, sound system, temperature, seating—I get a feel for how the room will work. I gauge the mood by how the students enter the auditorium. Are they quiet? Sullen? Wild? Unruly? Tired? I prefer crazy and crowded.

Second, I pick out a "victim." (Remember Dennis in chapter one?) In all of my assemblies I choose a student to feature. I have to pick just the right kid, of course. The noisiest section of the crowd is usually promising.

I watched the students tumble in and spotted him right away. Seated front and center, talking up a storm. Even while I was being introduced, this motor-mouth never stopped to breathe.

I asked him his name. Excited to be singled out, he yelled, "Jason." When laughter erupted throughout the audience, I knew I had the right guy.

I had some fun with Jason during the assembly and wasn't surprised to see him later hanging out at the cafeteria—still talking. As soon as he saw me, he ran over and gave me a big hug. Then he leaped up onto a table and started the crowd chanting, "Drilling time, drilling time. Let's drill Miles."

He dragged me to the opposite end of the cafeteria while a hundred or so kids followed, the crowd swelling by the minute. Everyone seemed to know what "drilling" meant but me. I knew I was in trouble, and Jason was the ringleader.

As the crowd surrounded us, Jason started making fun of me in the form of free-style rap. He rapped about my hair, nose, Dudley Do-Right chin, and polyester shirt (I didn't think it looked like polyester, but, oh well)—a hilarious rhyme with a beat that his friend spontaneously created, as the crowd urged him on. While everyone was laughing at my expense, I interrupted.

"Listen," I said, trying to be heard over their hilarity, "I'm impressed. Do you know how much talent it takes to pull this off? Do you realize how quick, creative, and organized Jason's mind must be?" I talked to them about the gifts buried inside of them, talents that haven't even had a chance to surface yet.

You try to make up a rhyme and put it to a beat—it's not easy. I saw in Jason a natural leader with creative talent, and I wanted those kids to know that each of them has the same raw potential inside. Someone just needs to dig it out.

UNEARTH THE GIFT

BURIED TREASURE

If you're going to discover your child's gifts or talents and help grow them, you have to believe those talents exist. Let me put any doubt to rest: The Bible says, "Each one has his own gift from God, one in this manner and another in that" (1 Corinthians 7:7).

God declares He has given each of us a gift that is uniquely our own. We can therefore confidently tell our young people that they each possess "good and perfect" gifts, given by "the Father of the heavenly lights, who does not change like shifting shadows" (James 1:17, NIV).

Is it real to you that God has tucked special talents inside your child? Maybe they're hard to see right now. Maybe you wonder if you'll ever find them. But look at your child's gift like buried treasure. It's there, somewhere underneath the dirt. Someone simply needs to believe in your child and in his or her gift enough to start digging for it.

Matthew 25 provides an illustration of how talents get buried—and how God wants them dug up and put to use.

A wealthy businessman took a long journey, leaving three servants in charge of his holdings. To each servant, the master allocated resources to manage, according to his individual gifts and abilities.

To one he gave five "talents"—that's a sum of money, but it's a handy coincidence for thinking about the gifts God has put in our kids. To another he gave two talents, and to another only one. Upon his return, the master asked each servant to explain what he had done with his talents. Through wise investments, the one with five had doubled his master's money. The one with two had two more. Both were rewarded generously and shared in the master's joy at seeing how their lives had prospered.

The third servant, however, simply gave back what he had been given. He hadn't wanted to risk his talent by investing it, so he buried it in the ground. His reward? Punishment—for wasting an opportunity and disobeying his master's instructions to invest his talent!

The unproductive servant's explanation was "I was afraid. . . ." Of what? Taking a risk? Rejection? Failure? His fear denied him the joy of his master.

I grieve when I see young people burying their talents. I know they're going to miss out on their Master's joy unless we help them dig up their gifts.

The dirt that hides talents comes in many forms. But if you know what kind of dirt it is, you can help uncover your child's talent.

BURIED IN DISCOURAGEMENT

A girl stopped me with a pointed question as I walked down a school hallway: "Are we as bad as they say?" She was referring to a recent media report that portrayed this student body in a very grim light. I watched a paralyzing discouragement settle over that school as students began to believe their bad press.

When adults quit believing in kids, the kids accept that negative judgment of their lives and sink to the occasion. They quit applying themselves. They settle for second best—or worse. When kids live with the burden of a bad reputation, labeled by people who usually don't know them, they abandon hope.

Discouragement emanates from discouraging surroundings. Kids from disadvantaged backgrounds often bury their talents in a hole of hopelessness and low expectations. But even kids who know they have gifts will do nothing with them when nothing is expected. They live down to low or no expectations. "For as [a man] thinketh in his heart, so is he" (Proverbs 23:7, KJV). If we lump teenagers together as losers, that's what most of them will become. Granted, some kids have messed up their lives badly, but that doesn't change the fact that God has gifted even those wounded kids with special talents. If someone would only believe that somewhere inside, buried treasure is hidden, their lives could be dramatically changed.

The girl who stopped me in the hall was really asking for someone to tell her, "You're OK." What I told her was, "You are more than OK. You are wonderful. As a matter of fact, you are special to

God and to me." I gave her a hug and she walked away smiling, as I prayed for God to continue to encourage her.

BURIED IN FEAR OF FAILURE

My daughter Kimmie is shy and cautious. She resists new situations and avoids drawing attention to herself. When she started school, we had to pry her off us to get her into the building. In first grade, four months passed before she would speak to her teacher.

I was excited when she announced she wanted to take gymnastics. But when we arrived for her first class, she hung on to me with all her might. "Here we go again," I thought, sadly.

I looked at all the cheerful parents around us and tried to identify with their aspirations for their children to compete in high school, college, or go to the Olympics. All I wanted was for my daughter to walk into class without clinging to me in terror.

The class lasted ninety minutes. For all ninety of those minutes Kimmie sat on the edge of the mat, getting up only to come talk to me. It was so painful to watch her, I had to fight back tears. "What is she so scared of?" I wondered. "What is holding her back?"

When she got up to run over to me, I gave her a hug and a kiss, then sent her back with encouragement to just give it a try. But still she sat on the edge watching, and wrestling with her own fears.

When the class was over, I was pleased to see the instructor take a few minutes to focus on Kimmie and let her try a few skills. Kimmie completed them all as well or better than most of the other girls, the whole time looking over her shoulder to see if I was watching. I could see that she is stronger and more athletic than she thinks.

My daughter was hindered tremendously by her fear of failure. Once she gained some confidence and realized she could actually do what was expected, she began to progress. One day she walked into class by herself. Before long, she was recommended for the advanced program!

The talent had been there all along, buried by her fear of failure. We just needed a couple of tools to dig it up—patience from me as her parent, and wisdom on the part of Kimmie's teacher in giving her a few minutes of individual attention and encouragement.

BURIED IN PEER PRESSURE

In some segments of our culture, it's not cool to do well in school. Hanging out in the halls, being late to class, or ditching altogether is cool. Only when it's too late do young people realize what a mistake they've made. I wish they could meet all the adults in the world who regret not having applied themselves in school when they were young—when they buried their talents under peer pressure.

BURIED IN NEGATIVITY

Nineteen-year-old Rochelle, a talented artist, was invited to apply for a job in the art department of a major Hollywood studio. When she told her parents, their response was "You're too young for that! You're not ready for a job like that. You're not even qualified. How will you manage to live in Los Angeles?"

While Rochelle was initially bursting with enthusiasm and confidence, her parents' fears deflated her excitement and kept her from applying for the job. Of course, they might have been right. She might not have been hired, or, if she was, she might have failed. But they launched into a problem-spotting mode rather than a problem-solving mode. They could have let her know how proud they were of her even getting this opportunity, then discussed their concerns. If their daughter still wanted to pursue the job, they could have prayed, helped her with her application and résumé, and trusted the Lord for the outcome. (By the way, that's the conclusion the parents came to later.)

HE IS ABLE

HOPE ALL THINGS

About three thousand years ago, a multitalented shepherd boy named David sat in the fields tending his sheep and writing music.

As the youngest of seven boys, David not only got his fill of getting picked on by his older brothers but his own father thought little of him.

Few people saw David's potential. His father, Jesse, "forgot" to call him in from the fields when the prophet Samuel visited their home in search of God's anointed king. When the teenage David volunteered to fight Goliath, King Saul, his brothers, and everyone in Israel's army within earshot told him he was too young. "Go home," they said. "Tend your sheep and play your songs. Leave men's work to men."

God, however, had a plan for David. David was not only destined to be a king but one of the most successful kings in history. As we all know, David did kill Goliath, was crowned king, and became one of the most published songwriters in history (the Psalms)!

We might look at our kids and doubt their abilities, or wonder about their seemingly insignificant jobs or incomprehensible experiences. Then again, who are we to minimize what God is teaching our children? He has a plan. He hears our prayers. He is exceedingly able and willing to turn our children's experiences into something positive, as the following verses verify:

> Now to Him who is able to do exceedingly abundantly above all that we ask or think, according to the power that works in us . . . (Ephesians 3:20).

> Now to Him who is able to keep you from stumbling, and to present you faultless before the presence of His glory with exceeding joy . . . (Jude 24).

ALWAYS HOPE

MORE THAN ENOUGH

The Bible says love "hopes all things" (1 Corinthians 13:7). Love looks on the positive side of things. Love sees things as they *can be* and not necessarily as they *are*.

Jesus once had five thousand hungry people to feed and few resources. When a young boy came to Him with five loaves and two fish, His disciples saw exactly that: five loaves and two fish. Not enough for a crumb per person.

But Jesus saw something different. God doesn't see what we see.

Jesus had the people sit down. Then He took a child's insignificant offering and made a miracle of it: "Jesus then took the loaves, gave thanks, and distributed to those who were seated as much as they wanted. He did the same with the fish. When they had all had enough to eat, He said to His disciples, 'Gather the pieces that are left over. Let nothing be wasted' " (John 6:11–12, NIV).

The boy gave all he had to the Lord, and God blessed it and multiplied it—with some left over. It was more than enough.

As young people look for their talents, all they need is the smallest sign of God-given ability. No matter how underdeveloped, a gift given back to God will be more than enough. Adults can help by looking for the smallest potential and foreseeing how God can turn it into something wonderful.

SEE THE GOOD

SEARCH FOR GOLD

No matter how much time my daughter Kelly spends cleaning her room, it's a mess ten minutes later. Junk and an array of "stuff" seem to ooze from the walls through some kind of supernatural reproduction. Either that or she has a secret roommate who trashes her room when we turn our backs.

On the other hand, Kelly shows great artistic talent. She draws prolifically—people in the family or animals from magazines. She makes cards for birthdays and holidays. There's always a drawing or sculpture somewhere underneath the junk. We just have to look. Sometimes, when I walk into her room, frustration overtakes me—until I spot that hidden artistic treasure. Somewhere, hidden beneath your child's messes and mistakes, there lie hidden talents and God-given gifts. You just need to look for them.

Here are some "digging tools" to help you in your search:

1. LOOSE YOUR CHILD'S GIFTS

My messy daughter is also the one who loves animals. One summer she conducted a class for the neighborhood kids on animals. She set up the class in her bedroom, complete with charts explaining the food chain and animal classifications from birds to reptiles. She made desks out of TV trays and a pointer for her charts out of five straws. She even gave assigned homework!

My wife and I recognize that one of her gifts is her extreme self-motivation in exploring new things. We have no idea where her gifts will lead, but we are excited that her interests continue to spark her performance in other areas. She is taking an art class right now—and learning to draw animals!

I don't ever want to limit the interests she pursues. We have no idea how God might choose to use her particular combination of passions and gifts, and I don't want be in the way when He does.

Remember, in Jesus' parable of the talents, the master gave each of his servants a different number of gifts. To one five, to another two, to another one, each according to his ability. What a shame it would have been for the five-talent servant to have invested only one of his talents. If the one-talent servant had invested his gift wisely, I have no doubt his master would have added more.

Look at David. He could write and play music, tend sheep, lead an army, and wield a slingshot with deadly accuracy. Every aspect of his abilities created the complete person God designed to be king of Israel.

Likewise, don't let your kid limit his capabilities. God wants to use every aspect of that multifaceted personality.

2. ENCOURAGE YOUR CHILD TO EXCEL

Rhino isn't what you might think—he is not a big, strong animal with a huge tusk on the front of his face. The Rhino I know walks around like he runs everything, kind of like the rhinos I've seen at the zoo. But this Rhino is a thirteen-year-old boy who stands only 5'4" and weighs 140 pounds.

When Ryan (Rhino) was twelve years old, he played on a summer Little League team and struck out 120 batters in twelve games. He struck out eighteen in one game alone. That's two per inning! In seventh grade he pitched for an eighth grade team and was voted Athlete of the Year. In spite of being smaller and younger than most of his competitors, there's no stopping Rhino or his athletic prowess.

Rhino started bowling at three, won his first tournament at eight, and has won eleven so far. His average score is 198, but he also holds the record for being the youngest person in San Diego to ever bowl a perfect 300.

Rhino is gifted. In every sport he plays, he excels. For someone so young, he has a wild ability to accept challenges and pursue excellence. He also acknowledges the source of his gift by praying before every game, dedicating his efforts to the Lord.

Now that Rhino has been pegged as a champion ballplayer and bowler, I hope he will never limit himself. His discipline and desire to excel could splash over to many other areas as he matures.

However your child is gifted, whether in sports, academics, arts, or music, encourage him to excel. Maybe your child's gifts are less measurable. He might have the gift of compassion, of being friendly, or of helping others. Even then, encourage him to do what he does to the best of his ability. "Whatever you do," the Bible says, "do it heartily, as to the Lord and not to men" (Colossians 3:23).

3. RECOGNIZE THEIR GIFTS

The easiest way to recognize a child's talents is to look for what comes easiest—or what grabs his or her interest. Does your child display a natural bent for singing, dancing, or playing a sport? Does he or she enjoy writing, music, math, or science? Sit down with each of your children and compile a list of their favorite activities. Keep the list and refer to it as you pray and guide your child. These interests might not coincide with your child's adult occupation. Then again, they might!

My sister loved makeup and looking pretty. She'd get up at six in the morning just to have the bathroom to herself for an hour before school. We used to tease her about it, but no more. Today she runs a successful cosmetology business.

Think back a few years. If someone had conscientiously studied you when you were young and listed all your interests, what would be on it? Can you look back and see interests you wish someone had encouraged you to pursue? Do you have talents that remind you of those in your child?

When I was young, I loved to argue—especially with my family—about anything and everything. If the sun was up, I had to come up with some big argument about how it wasn't really because by the time the light actually reaches us, the sun has already moved. Even if I had no idea what I was talking about, I invented a reason to argue. My dad used to shake his head and tell me I should be a lawyer.

I can see now that God was preparing a preacher who would be ready to argue for the sake of the Gospel. He was training me to present the Good News with passion, conviction, and urgency, not wanting anyone to be lost. I'm still competitive and hate to lose a debate. To me, every sermon is an argument with someone who believes the devil's point of view. That's an argument I don't want to lose. With hell waiting to swallow up lost souls, the stakes are too high to lose.

My daughter takes after me, adding a "but" to the end of everything I say. She says she wants to be a lawyer. Although I think she's in it for the money, I plan to encourage her. (At least I'll get some reimbursement for all the "but-what-abouts" she's put me through).

4. ASK OTHERS ABOUT YOUR CHILD'S GIFTS

When you compile that list of your child's talents and strengths, ask other people what they see. Friends, relatives, mentors, teachers, coaches, employers—anyone who spends time with your child—often see things that you won't. It's just another way of encouraging your child to see his gifts. After all, most of those people aren't obligated to say nice things about your child. Your child can't say, "But *you're* my mother" when *they* offer encouragement.

5. LOOK TO THE FUTURE

Despite being shy, my daughter loves to sing. She sings in the bathtub, in front of mirrors, all through concerts. I know that she longs to be a part of a choir or small singing group. When we encourage her to join up, she says she's not good enough. Compared to the performers she watches and listens to, she's not. But so what! That's the wrong standard for comparison.

We want everything in a hurry—including success and ability. I remind my daughter that professional performers weren't born appearing on television, making millions of dollars, and singing in front of vast audiences. Most of them did for years exactly what she is doing now—dreaming, and singing in front of a mirror. A more valid standard of comparison is the progress an individual achieves after making the effort to work at something he or she loves.

A child's talents are seeds that will grow only when they are planted, watered, and allowed time to blossom.

When I say that we can often spot God's gifts in what a young person loves to do, that doesn't necessarily mean he'll be a star in that area. And you know what? He doesn't need to be. What he needs is a desire to do his best. Natural talent is less important than determination.

JUST DO IT!
INVESTING IN YOUR CHILD'S INTERESTS

Once you uncover your child's talents, what's next? How can you help your child double his talents so he enters into God's joy?

Attention to little things facilitates the bigger goal of finding God's calling on a child's life. As I watched my daughter sit on the edge of that gymnastics mat, I wondered if I had done something to cause her reluctance to join in. There is no worse feeling than a gnawing unease that you might somehow have hindered your child. And if you think about it long enough, you'll drive yourself crazy coming up with things you could have done differently. God's good news is that you can make a decision *now* to change your course of action. As you seek to help your child find God's greatness for his life, this is when it gets fun.

Here are a few ideas to help you develop your child's talents:

1. ENCOURAGE RISK-TAKING

"If you are going to learn from your mistakes and failures, you first have to be willing to make them," author Ron Jenson says. "You must be willing to take risks. Don't play it safe; learn to live on the edge." When you fall, fall forward. But don't be afraid to try.

Sitting in a gymnasium before a school assembly, I noticed an amazing haircut. On one side of a young man's head the hair faded from top to bottom, while on the other side an amusement park was etched onto his scalp. Cut into his hair was the outline of a Ferris wheel and a train! I called him over to get a closer look. There was even a "You are here" sign with a map to his house.

I asked him who his incredibly gifted barber was, and he proudly told me, "I did it myself." He went on to describe how he held a mirror in one hand and clippers in the other to create his work of art. It was such good advertising that other kids—and even some teachers—started paying for their own custom-designed haircuts. He had turned his unique talent into a business.

Can you imagine the risk that kid took cutting his own hair? He told me he was a little nervous at first. He didn't know how his new look would be received. But he took the risk, and it paid off. It reminds me of a sign I saw in a northern California school: "If you are not willing to go too far, you will never know how far you can go."

2. PROD TO ACTION

Just Do It! Our young people need to hear this message loud and clear: *Got a gift? Use it. Even if you're no good. Even if you don't progress quickly. Just do it.*

The Bible reminds us not to despise small beginnings (Zechariah 4:10). A slow or tough-slogging beginning doesn't mean there won't be a victorious ending. Usually the opposite is true.

Remind your child that God has committed himself to working with her to develop her talents. Tell her what the apostle Paul knew to be a great truth: "Being confident of this very thing, that He who has begun a good work in you will complete it until the day of Christ Jesus" (Philippians 1:6). Your kid needs to be encouraged to try, even when trying is difficult, even when failure is likely. Reassure your child that it's OK to fail as long as he doesn't lie on the ground. He can get up and try again. A righteous man can fall even seven times, the Bible says, and gets up again.

Hidden talents and untapped potential begin to shine when we encourage our young people to go for it.

3. FOCUS ON STRENGTH

When I ask kids what they want to be when they grow up, I typically get, "I don't know," or they say, "I want to be a doctor, lawyer, play football, and own a business." It's a rare kid who gives me only one thing as the object of his focus.

When I was a youth pastor, I struggled with the administration part of the ministry, but I was excited about teaching and preaching. A good friend, observing my frustration, counseled me, "Don't ask God to bless what you do. Instead, spend time doing what God blesses." His counsel changed my life. I delegated many of the administrative details to people gifted in that area, and focused on my gifts of preaching and teaching. Another way of looking at this: there's a personal growth principle that says we should spend 80 percent of our time in our areas of strength and 20 percent in our areas of weakness. While that principle is harder to apply to a child or teen—because we all need mastery of basics in a lot of areas—the point is the same: encourage excellence in a few specific areas. Once young people discover their talents, our job is to encourage them to focus on developing those talents.

SET THE GOAL
WHAT IS GOOD ENOUGH?

During my fourth year with the San Diego Chargers, the team brought in four rookie defensive backs to take the place of us "old guys."

Defensive backs are supposed to be versatile, athletic, and fast. We had to keep up with the fastest players on the opposing team, and do it while running backwards, sideways, and in circles. We had to be prepared to hit linemen who weighed three hundred pounds and tackle running backs who ate nails for breakfast. We were required to do it all. That's especially true for cornerbacks, who are usually smaller and faster.

Tight ends are offensive players who are bigger and generally slower than defensive backs—and you can figure out what that means: A cornerback should never let a tight end outrun him. Once as we watched films to review one game, we all saw Terry, a fast and aggressive cornerback, chase but not catch a slower, less athletic tight end. Not good.

The coach stopped the film, turned on the lights, and slowly spun around in his chair. He searched for Terry among the thirty defensive players. We all turned and looked too, knowing Terry was going to get it. The room hushed.

The coach glared, then yelled, "Terry, is that as fast as you can run?"

Terry was paralyzed. The coach raised his voice a notch and yelled again, "Terry, is that as fast as you can run?"

If Terry said, "Yes sir," the coach would have answered, "Son, that is not good enough." If Terry answered, "No, coach" he still would have heard, "That's not good enough."

Terry finally answered, "No, coach, it's not the fastest I can run, but I was hurt." Guess what the coach said? "Son, that's not good enough."

The coach suspected Terry was holding back, that in spite of his injury he could have given more. While hollering sounds harsh—

don't try it at home—an experienced coach could spot that Terry wasn't giving his all. He knew how to pull a few more ounces of energy out of his player.

What *would have* been good enough for our coach? One hundred percent of our very best effort. Anything less simply wasn't good enough.

Our kids need to be told what "good enough" is. To me, "good enough" is their very best effort.

Katie came tumbling down the stairs, paper in hand. Grabbing her school backpack, she was about to stuff her report in when her mother intercepted it and asked, "Are you finished?"

"Yeah! I'm all done. I can go outside now." The sound of kids on the street made her want to hurry.

Her mother, after reading over the paper, handed it back to her. "This is not the best you can do," she said, and proceeded to point out several places where the report needed to be rewritten and improved.

An unhappy Katie headed back upstairs and reworked her paper until it passed inspection. However disgruntled Katie was at having to stay in longer to do her best work, she was even more excited the next day when she came home with an A on her paper.

Requiring the best from your child takes wisdom. Your child doesn't need a mom or dad or a teacher who is never satisfied. Pray for wisdom in striking the balance between pushing hard and riding easy. No kid has to win all the time. He just has to give his best effort. Kids don't have to *be* the best, just *do* their best.

A coach knows when to push a player harder because he spends his life watching that player play. When you're engaged with your child and slogging through life alongside him, studying his efforts, supporting his weaknesses, you'll have a good idea of when to prod and when to pull back.

BELIEVE IN THEM
BE A CHEERLEADER

During my four years in Pee Wee football, my parents attended almost every game. Some of my teammates, however, never saw their folks at a game the entire four years. My parents were there through high school and college, driving as long as ten hours to see a game. When I made it to the NFL, they couldn't attend every game but they did fly across the country to see several of them. I could count on them as my most faithful fans. Now, even though I'm not playing, they are still cheering for me.

I try to follow their example in my own family. Almost every week, I sit at my daughter's gymnastic class just to give her a thumbs up. No matter what my kids do, I try to be there as often as possible to cheer them on.

They know their mother and I will be their biggest fans and most faithful cheerleaders. As parents, that's our role.

Believing in our children—and carrying out that belief through our prayers, words, and actions—unleashes them to be all they can be. It's our privilege to cheer them forward.

After all, if we don't believe in our children, who will?

Thank you for selecting a book from
BETHANY HOUSE PUBLISHERS

Bethany House Publishers is a ministry of Bethany Fellowship
International, an interdenominational, nonprofit organization
committed to spreading the Good News of Jesus Christ around
the world through evangelism, church planting, literature
distribution, and care for those in need. Missionary training is
offered through Bethany College of Missions.

Bethany Fellowship International is a member of the National
Association of Evangelicals and subscribes to its statement of
faith. If you would like further information, please contact:

Bethany Fellowship International
6820 Auto Club Road
Minneapolis, MN 55438 USA